A GUIDE TO GREEN NEW

ON LINE

A GUIDE TO
GREEN
NEW JERSEY

*Nature Walks
in the Garden State*

LUCY D. ROSENFELD
MARINA HARRISON

RUTGERS UNIVERSITY PRESS
New Brunswick, New Jersey, and London

Library of Congress Cataloging-in-Publication Data

Rosenfeld, Lucy D.

A guide to green New Jersey : nature walks in the garden state : forests, beaches, vineyards, battlefields, rail trails, marshes, orchards, canals, gardens, and more / Lucy D. Rosenfeld and Marina Harrison.

      p.   cm.

Includes index.

ISBN 0-8135-3230-2 (pbk : alk. paper)

1. Hiding—New Jersey—Guidebooks. 2. Nature study—New Jersey—Guidebooks. 3. New Jersey—Guidebooks. I. Harrison, Marina, 1939– II. Title

GV199.42.N5 R67 2003

917.4904'44—dc21   2002012413

British Cataloging-in-Publication information is available from the British Library.

Manufactured in the United States of America

CONTENTS

Map of New Jersey with Walking Sites   ix

Introduction   xi

1 • RINGWOOD REGION   I
*A Lakeside Walk, Strolling through a Botanical Garden,
and Exploring an Eclectic Estate*

2 • RAMAPO REGION   5
*Birding through a Former Celery Farm and Woodsy Environmental
Center, Hiking in the Ramapos, and Climbing on an Off-Season
Ski Slope*

3 • HUDSON REGION   9
*A Hudson River Walk in the Dramatic Palisades, a Nature Center
with a Quarry Boardwalk, and Birding in a Marsh*

4 • PATERSON REGION   14
Romantic Vistas: The Great Falls, Castle Ruins, and Mountain Trails

5 • MONTCLAIR REGION   18
*Nature Tended and Wild: Cherry Trees, a Picturesque Cemetery,
Formal Gardens, and a Nature Preserve*

6 • LIBERTY STATE PARK   24
The Great City Skyline: Scenic Walks on the Hudson's Jersey Side

7 • GREAT SWAMP REGION   28
Wildlife Walks: Songbirds, Owls, Butterflies, and Waterfowl

8 • MILLBURN REGION   33
*Hawk Watching in a Wooded Reservation, Walking in an Arboretum,
and Deep Woods with a Forgotten Village*

9 • BERNARDSVILLE REGION   38
*Walking through Four Inviting Gardens: Walled Victoriana, Hillside
Rock Gardens, a Naturalistic Delight, and a Willowy Arboretum*

10• MORRISTOWN REGION   43
Patriot's Path: Great Hikes through Morristown's Historic Woods and Lakelands

11• MOUNTAIN LAKES AND BOONTON REGION   48
Images of Impressionism: A Reflective Lakeside Walk, Carpets of Wildflowers, and a Sun-Dappled Wooded Landscape

12• FROM JENNY JUMP TO SPARTA   53
Rural New Jersey: Mountains, a Ghost Lake, a Scenic Rail Trail, and a Historic Village

13• THE NORTHWEST CORNER OF SUSSEX COUNTY   58
New Jersey High Points: A Ravine, a Waterfall, a Mountain Trail, and a Lake

14• WARREN COUNTY   64
Delaware Water Gap: Four Samplings of a Spectacular Region

15• ALLAMUCHY AND WEST   69
Off the Beaten Track in Western New Jersey: Walking across a Dam, through Woodland Preserves, and Wildlife Havens

16• CHESTER AREA   74
Exploring the Black River

17• CLINTON AREA   79
Green Hunterdon: Walking through a Tranquil River Gorge, a Fitness Forest Trail, a Naturalistic Arboretum, and a Lakeside Park

18• RINGOES AND MILFORD REGIONS   84
Vineyard Walks: Western New Jersey's Prettiest Wineries

19• SOMERSET COUNTY   88
Winter Getaway: Indoor and Outdoor Pleasures

20• DELAWARE AND RARITAN CANAL REGION   93
Along a Peaceful Canal and through a Rose Garden

21• ROUTE 1, MIDDLESEX COUNTY AREA   97
Well-Kept Secrets: Nature Walks in a Bamboo Forest, a University Woodland, and a Lakeside Bird Sanctuary

22• PRINCETON   101
*Princeton Pleasures: Campus Sculpture Walk, University Gardens,
a Park-cum-Arboretum, and a Historic Cemetery*

23• MERCER COUNTY   107
*Along the Delaware: A Historic Park, a Canal Walk, a Corn Maze,
and a Medicinal Trail*

24• HAMILTON TOWNSHIP   113
A Trio of Parks: Sculpture, Flowers, and Bikeways

25• NORTH TIP OF THE JERSEY SHORE   119
*Exploring Sandy Hook: An Ocean Beach, a Holly Forest,
and a Bay Island*

26• EASTERN MONMOUTH COUNTY   124
*Off the North Shore: A Salt Marsh, an Arboretum, a Dogwood Trail,
and a Garden with a Past*

27• FREEHOLD REGION   129
*A Battlefield, a Reservoir Loop, a Meadow Walk on a Rail Trail,
and an Abandoned Village*

28• LAKEWOOD AREA   133
*Lakeside Pleasures: Biking and Hiking Lakeside Loops
and a Georgian Campus*

29• TOMS RIVER REGION   137
Coastal Pleasures: Islands, Oceanside, Bayside, Bogside

30• THE PINE BARRENS   141
*Cranberry Bogs in the Pine Barrens: Double Trouble State Park
and Lebanon State Forest*

31• PEMBERTON REGION   146
*Nature's Color: A Boardwalk through Wooded Wetlands,
a Great Rail Trail, a Waterside Ravine, and a Giant Corn Maze*

32• WHARTON STATE FOREST   151
Trails and Vistas in the Pine Barrens

33• CENTRAL JERSEY COAST   156
Hidden Bikeways along the Shore: Birds and Marshes in Brigantine

34• ATLANTIC COUNTY   162

Short Walks near Atlantic City: A Lakeside Loop, Exploring a Coastal Island, and 400,000 Orchids

35• CAPE MAY COUNTY   165

New Jersey's Southern Coastline: A Boardwalk, a Seawall, and Sandy Paths through Remote Marshes and along Coastal Inlets

36• CAPE MAY   169

New Jersey's Southern Tip: Birds, Butterflies, Breakwater, and Beaches

37• DELAWARE BAY REGION   174

Biking the Remote South Jersey Coast: An Island, Salt Marshland, Sandy Beaches, and a Historic Lighthouse

38• SOUTH-CENTRAL NEW JERSEY   178

Treats in Three Rural Counties: A Spectacular State Park, a Craft Village, an Arboretum, and a Remote Forest

39• DELAWARE RIVER REGION   183

The Mouth of the Delaware: Historic Sites and Water Views

40• EAST OF PHILADELPHIA   187

A Forest, a Native American Reservation, a Freshwater Tidal Marsh, and an Old Apple Orchard

Some Additional Green Sites to Explore   192

Choosing an Outing   196

Photo Credits   201

Index   203

1 • Ringwood Region
2 • Ramapo Region
3 • Hudson Region
4 • Paterson Region
5 • Montclair Region
6 • Liberty State Park
7 • Great Swamp Region
8 • Millburn Region
9 • Bernardsville Region
10 • Morristown Region
11 • Mountain Lakes–Boonton
Region
12 • From Jenny Jump
to Sparta
13 • The Northwest Corner
of Sussex County
14 • Warren County
15 • Allamuchy and West
16 • Chester Area
17 • Clinton Area
18 • Ringoes and Milford
Regions
19 • Somerset County
20 • Delaware and Raritan
Canal Region
21 • Route 1, Middlesex
County Area
22 • Princeton
23 • Mercer County
24 • Hamilton Township
25 • North Tip of the
Jersey Shore
26 • Eastern Monmouth
County
27 • Freehold
Region
28 • Lakewood Area
29 • Toms River
Region
30 • The Pine
Barrens
31 • Pemberton
Region
32 • Wharton
State
Forest
33 • Central
Jersey
Coast
34 • Atlantic
County
35 • Cape May
County
36 • Cape May
37 • Delaware
Bay Region
38 • South-Central
New Jersey
39 • Delaware River Region
40 • East of Philadelphia

INTRODUCTION

A Word to Our Readers
and How to Use This Book

New Jersey is a state of surprises. Researching these walks turned out to be an eye-opening experience, even though we thought we knew the state well, having lived in the region for decades. Despite its proximity to major urban areas, and its high population density, New Jersey has dozens of absolutely marvelous natural areas and preserved spaces. In fact, we discovered that this is a state with an unusually large amount of undeveloped or what we call "saved" land.

And there is more all the time. Just this year, $8.1 million for land preservation in the state was approved in Congress; allocations are for Cape May's National Wildlife Refuge, the Newark Watershed, and the Edwin B. Forsythe National Wildlife Refuge, among other sites. In addition, the state itself has several programs for restoring forests and other natural areas, such as the replanting of white cedar forests. Several private organizations, including the National Audubon Society and groups that are buying farmland to save it from urban sprawl, have had notable success. We applaud all of these efforts, for we have a beautiful state.

Surprisingly, because we found so many wonderful areas we could have included in compiling the walks and outings in this book, we had to pick and choose which ones to use. At the risk of sounding like the tourist board, we note enthusiastically that New Jersey's landscape has something for everyone who enjoys walking, from Atlantic seashore to rugged mountains, rolling farmland to winding canals, historic trails to formal gardens, bird-filled marshes to hardwood forests, pine barrens to fragrant vineyards and orchards. Following our own tastes for a variety of terrain and experience, we decided to compile not just a list of major wilderness areas and the hikes therein, but to search out a panoply of experiences for our hikers, bikers, beachcombers, gardeners, power walkers, and strollers of all kinds.

Here are a few guidelines for using this book and enjoying the outings described in it. You will find at the beginning of the book a map bearing forty numbers. Each number represents an area that includes three or four recommended sites. We suggest that you choose the region you would like to explore, and then read the descriptions of these several walks or bicycle rides before setting out. Perhaps you will want to take several days to explore each section; in some cases, all of the outings will fit into one day's excursion.

Walking or biking in this region of the Northeast is, of course, most enjoyable in spring and autumn, when foliage is at its loveliest, the temperatures are perfect, and the bugs are busy elsewhere. These are our most beautiful seasons. But you will also be able to do almost all of these outings in summer, if it is not too hot; some of them—like the oceanside walks—are particularly wonderful in steamy weather. And you'll find that pine forests and beaches, for example, are great places to visit in the cold of winter.

We recommend picking up printed trail guides, if available at the entrances to wooded hiking areas. Walkers should always follow the appropriate color markings that have been painted on the trees along the paths in many forest areas. These markings are known as "blazes" and are used to identify trails. You cannot get lost if you follow them. Avoid marshes, low-lying areas, and deep woods in the height of mosquito and tick season. Do pay strict attention to signs in wilderness areas; avoid "hunting permitted" regions in the fall. And, as all walkers know, avoid poison ivy and poison oak!

We think you'll find all of our outings inviting; we have tried to choose sites that have little or no traffic sounds, so that you can hear the birdcalls and feel that you have escaped civilization for just a little while. Some of these sites are remote. Always lock your car wherever you leave it, and we recommend taking a companion through the most remote areas.

We have included some pertinent information: hours that a site is open when relevant, parking when available, fees when required, and telephone numbers so you can call ahead to check on conditions if you wish. At the end of the book you'll find an index with the names of all of the sites, and our guide to choosing an outing, according to your tastes and interests. We have identified walks that are particularly nice to do with children, those that are accessible for wheelchairs and kids' strollers, trips that are best by bicycle, and those that are a bit too difficult to hike unless you are very fit.

Finally, we want to wish you as much enjoyment on these wonderful outings as we have had.

A GUIDE TO GREEN NEW JERSEY

1·
RINGWOOD
REGION

Shepherd Lake, Ringwood State Park.

A Lakeside Walk,
Strolling through a Botanical Garden,
and Exploring an Eclectic Estate

⚜ HOW TO GET THERE

Shepherd Lake (Ringwood State Park)

From the New York State Thruway, take Route 17 north. Follow signs for Ringwood. You'll see signs for Shepherd Lake before you reach Ringwood. (You'll be on Morris Avenue and turning onto Shepherd Lake Road.)

Skylands Botanical Garden

The garden is located in Ringwood and can be reached from Morris Avenue as above, or from Route 208 to Route 511. Take the second right, Sloatsburg Road; Morris Avenue is 4.5 miles farther. Follow signs to Skylands.

Ringwood Manor

You'll come to the entrance to Ringwood Manor just after Shepherd Lake on Morris Avenue.

Shepherd Lake is 1,000 feet above sea level, nestled in the Ramapo Mountains. A spring-fed lake, it is blue and cool, and a particularly nice place to walk around outside of the usual summer season, when it is a popular bathing spot. It is particularly pretty in the fall when the many trees turn beautiful colors and are reflected in the lake's clear waters.

After you park, you'll see a quaint stone chapel on a slight rise above the lake, and a boathouse on the water's edge. Enter the trail around the lake near the boathouse, and follow red markers. (This is the Ringwood-Ramapo Trail.) It is a pretty path, both woodsy and easy to walk on, and the lake itself is a pleasure to look at. After a while the path turns into the woods and becomes steeper before leveling off again. This can be a hike of more than an hour, bringing you all the way to another body of water known as Swan Pond, and circling back again to Shepherd Lake, if you wish. Pick up a trail map at the boathouse. It is possible to walk all the way to our next destination on this trail.

Shepherd Lake is part of Ringwood State Park. Grounds are open from dawn to dusk year-round. Telephone: 973-962-7031.

Skylands Botanical Garden is New Jersey's state botanical garden, and it is aptly named. It sits at the top of New Jersey, high above most of the land in the state. It was once a grand—but quite informal—estate, with elegant Tudor-style buildings, long allées of trees, delightful gardens, and great vistas. Some 125 acres are here to be explored. You'll find a crab-apple walk—magnificent in springtime—and both formal and naturalistic plantings. An occasional statue graces the grounds.

Skylands was the home of Francis Lynde Stetson, a New York lawyer, who hired a protégé of Frederic Law Olmsted to design his "Sky Farm." Samuel Parsons did a wonderful job combining formal allées with sweeping lawns and wooded areas, but it was Clarence McKenzie Lewis, the next owner, who turned the estate into a botanical garden. During the 1920s Lewis began bringing specimen trees and plantings from all over the world to Skylands. Lewis considered the color, texture, form, and even fragrance of each plant so that it would be part of a harmonious whole. In the 1960s the state of New Jersey purchased the property and in 1984 designated the 94 acres around the mansion as the official botanical garden of the state. A descriptive guide and map are available at the Visitor Center.

A visit at Skylands should begin at the Center and include the Annual Garden, the Azalea Garden, Magnolia Garden, and Lilac Garden (in spring), the Peony Garden (late May), the Octagonal Garden (a lovely rock garden with pool and fountain), Winter Garden (with 30 varieties of evergreens), Crab Apple Vista (two double rows of trees), Bog Garden, Swan Pond, Wildflower Garden, Heather Garden, and the greenhouses. You can also walk into the wooded areas and visit the sculpture area, where statues representing the Four Continents are posed in a semicircle next to the woods. This is only a brief outline of the many delights of a visit to Skylands; a walk here is an experience that will awaken all of your senses.

Skylands is open daily, year-round, from 9 A.M. to dusk. Admission is charged in summertime. Tours are available daily every half hour. Telephone: 973-962-9534.

Ringwood Manor is nearby, and has a very different ambience. Ringwood is set in the hilly terrain of the Ramapo Mountains. It is part rural retreat with sculpture garden and part European-style garden. A National Historic site, it is a good place to walk and to enjoy a magnificent landscape filled with giant trees, stone walls, formal gardens, forest, lake, and orchards—as well as statuary.

Before the Revolutionary War iron was discovered here, and up until the end of World War I, Ringwood was a center of iron mining and munitions. It was home to Robert Erskine, General Washington's offical army mapmaker; he is buried here. The mansion that is still standing was built in 1854 and became the country estate of Cooper Hewitt, an iron magnate. His mansion, with notable art and antiques, is open to the public on certain days. (Telephone for information.) Descendants of Hewitt decided to landscape a portion of the 33,000 acres of land and to use classical designs seen during their European travels. Versailles was a major influence. The results are a mix of formal and naturalistic landscapes, with allées and formal terraces and walls, as well as large areas of prisitine landscape left in a natural state. You'll find statuary—ranging from classical figures (some reportedly from the Bishop's Palace at Avignon), to odd sphinxes, to curious constructions of wrought iron—adorning the estate. There is a geometrically divided, stone-walled and terraced hillside that will particularly delight children. This is an eccentric and fascinating estate, with ample room for walking and exploring.

Ringwood Manor is open year-round, but the gardens are best in spring and summer. In season there is a fee for parking. Telephone: 973-962-7031.

IN THE VICINITY
Wawayanda State Park
Wawayanda State Park offers serious hikers magnificent wooded trails to explore. Although there are areas in the park for boating and swimming, the forested sections of the park are remote and fairly rough, particularly in the Hemlock Ravine Natural Area. There are several recommended hikes within this wilderness (including a beautiful trail to Terrace Pond); be sure to get a map before setting out.

Long Pond Ironworks State Park
Long Pond Ironworks State Park contains not only a scenic wooded parkland, but also a historic village where ironworks once operated. A most unusual three-mile hike brings you into an eighteenth-century setting, as well as picturesque Greenwood Lake.

2·
RAMAPO
REGION

The Celery Farm.

*Birding through a Former Celery Farm
and Woodsy Environmental Center,
Hiking in the Ramapos, and
Climbing on an Off-Season Ski Slope*

🐚 HOW TO GET THERE

Celery Farm Natural Area (Fyke Nature Center)

From Route 17 in Allendale, exit at East Allendale Avenue (west). Turn right onto Franklin Turnpike (north). After the first cross street, followed by three houses on your right, you'll find a small parking area and a sign indicating a Green Acre site.

Ramapo County Reservation

From Route 17, go north; exit at Ramapo Avenue (west) to Route 202 south. Follow signs to park entrance.

Campgaw Mountain Ski Area

The ski area is located within the Ramapo County Reservation. From the parking area in the reservation retrace your steps back to Route 202 and follow signs to Campgaw Mountain Ski Area.

The Ramapo River Valley and surrounding region provide many wonderful sites for enjoying nature at its greenest, from wooded plains to hilly sites with glorious vistas. A trading post was established here as early as 1710, attracting squatters, including a group that combined Native American, African American, and European ethnicities. These Ramapo Mountain people—some of whose descendants are still in the region—lived here in virtual isolation.

Much of the area is still quite unspoiled, in some places even wild; indeed, in the vast Ramapo County Reservation you are unlikely to meet many visitors, especially at times when there is neither camping nor skiing, two of the park's popular activities.

The outing we propose includes a secluded birding retreat in the Allendale region just south of the Ramapos, and a vast, rugged parkland with many hiking options. The two we describe—around a picturesque pond and up a ski slope (after the snow has completely melted)—are quite tame, but feel free to explore the more rugged terrain!

🐦 **The Celery Farm Natural Area** (also known as the Allendale Celery Farm or Fyke Nature Center) is a hidden treasure that few—outside of its immediate neighbors—even know about. (In fact, there are no signs pointing to it until you're actually in its small parking area.) This totally uncommercial retreat is a paradise both for the many bird species that thrive here (some 231 at last count) and for their viewers. Including more than one hundred acres of freshwater marsh and woodlands, and no structures to speak of besides a few discrete little wooden platforms for bird watching, it is a natural oasis for all its creatures. A lake, complete with frogs, fish, and water birds, is at the center, surrounded by lush vegetation and woods. Trees draped with climbing vines emerge from the marshes, their lower branches touching the still water, creating the languid ambience of a swamp garden in the South.

There are few remaining signs of the celery farm that existed here in the late nineteenth century. Where the celery plants once grew are wetlands surrounded by masses of brilliant wildflowers, mostly yellow mustardseed and purple loosestrife. After the farm fell into disrepair, it was converted into a Green Acres site for viewing birds in a serene environment. Today the nature center is cared for by a group of eager volunteers who maintain the site and keep a careful log of its wildlife.

Before embarking on your walk, pick up a small brochure available right at the entrance. In remarkable detail it lists all the varieties of birds to look for—from loons, cormorants, herons, and swans to pheasants, cranes, gulls, sandpipers, owls, terns, woodpeckers, even hawks and vultures—and indeed, how likely each is to appear at any given time.

A woodsy walking trail winds around the lake, stopping en route to the three main bird viewing areas overlooking the water. If you go at a leisurely pace, it will take you about 45 minutes to walk all the way around the lake, not including any birding you might wish to do along the way. (Don't forget to bring your binoculars!)

This is a surprisingly quiet place, considering your proximity to surrounding pockets of suburbia, and you are unlikely to hear more than the sounds of chirping or squawking birds. Indeed, few people come here at all, especially during the week. After completing the loop and returning to your car, you will feel as though you've had a real reprieve from the usual hustle and bustle of modern life.

The Fyke Nature Center is open daily, year-round, from dawn to dusk. There is no charge. For further information (or to phone in any exotic variety of bird you may have spotted which is not listed) call 201-327-3470.

A few miles directly north, off Route 202 in the gently mountainous Ramapo region, lies the **Ramapo County Reservation.** This is a vast, 2,000-acre preserve of diverse habitats, ranging from woods and open fields to highlands, marshes, swamps, and lakes, and the Ramapo River itself. There are more than eight miles of hiking trails from which to explore this wilderness, to view its wildlife (there are about 200 species of birds), and to enjoy many scenic vistas. And if you come in spring, you'll see flowering dogwoods, pink azaleas, and mountain laurel.

After you leave your car in the parking lot (and pick up a trail guide, if one is available), head straight ahead, into the woods. A little bridge takes you over the narrow Ramapo River to a wide path leading to Scarlet Oak Pond. For a fairly short (little more than a mile) walk, you can encircle this pretty pond and its surrounding meadow laden with wildflowers. For a longer (about five-mile) and especially scenic hike with sweeping vistas from a high ridge, proceed on the trail uphill, crossing a stream with huge boulders, to MacMillan Reservoir. From this foresty site you eventually loop back down and around the pond.

The **Campgaw Ski Area** is situated within the park, and you can get there by following certain hiking trails, but we recommend taking your car and parking it directly at the base of the mountain. The Ramapo Mountains are not particularly high, and the vertical drop here is not more than 800 feet, making this not too strenuous a hike, even for families with children. (In fact, because of its gentle slopes, Campgaw is popular with families.) When you walk up the grassy hillside you'll be rewarded with a magnificent panoramic view of the entire region.

The Ramapo Reservation is open year-round, from dawn to dusk. There is no entrance fee for hiking. Telephone: 201-825-1388.

IN THE VICINITY

James A. McFaul Environmental Center

Not far away from the Ramapo Reservation is a very lovely place to walk, particularly with small children. Originally an 81-acre pig farm, it became a park and animal shelter/zoo in 1962. Here you'll find a lovely combination of gardens, waterfowl, boardwalk and observation deck, animals up-close, and woodsy trails. You can't do better than this for a not-too-long outing with the family; everyone will find something nice to do or see here. Pick up a trail guide at the headquarters. The Center is located at Crescent Avenue (north of Route 208), Wyckoff. Telephone: 201-891-5571.

3·
HUDSON
REGION

Walk along the Hudson.

A Hudson River Walk in the Dramatic
Palisades, a Nature Center with a Quarry
Boardwalk, and Birding in a Marsh

 HOW TO GET THERE

Palisades Shore Path

Take exit 1 on the Palisades Parkway. Follow signs to Englewood Boat Basin to walk north. Or exit 3 at Alpine Boat Basin to walk south.

Top of the Palisades Walk (Palisades Interstate Park)

Use stairway at western end of George Washington Bridge for southern end entrance, or enter at pedestrian bridge between exits 3 and 4 on the Palisades Parkway.

Flat Rock Brook Nature Center

Take Route 4, and exit at Jones Road, the first exit after the George Washington Bridge. Turn right on Van Nostrand Avenue, Englewood, and go to the top of the hill. For Jones Road Park, go several blocks farther on Jones Road and park along the road.

Overpeck Park

Take Fort Lee Road from Fort Lee west through Leonia, just past Grand Avenue, to entrance on left (near stables).

One of the most spectacular scenic areas in the state, and indeed in the nation, these Palisades—great rock cliffs descending into the grand Hudson River—are ideal for walkers both above and below. Whether you are wending your way on the narrow path a stone's throw from the water's edge below the Palisades, or way up on top looking out at the river's expanse and the city beyond, this is a glorious site to walk. The outings suggested here are ideal for lovers of scenery and for birders; here you will find river views, geological wonders, wildflowers, and waterbirds, and—in contrast—city views and boats passing by.

These majestic, towering cliffs are among the great natural wonders of our region. Formed about 190 million years ago and extending for some 40 miles north along New Jersey's and New York's shorelines, they were "saved" from excessive rock quarrying by an Interstate Park Commission in 1900, and by the Rockefeller interest in preserving in parkland one of the most beautiful areas in the East. The **Palisades Shore Path** takes the walker from the Englewood Boat Basin (where you can leave your car) north for more than ten miles. (If you don't want to retrace your steps you can loop around by climbing some steep steps here and there and returning via a roadway on the cliff above the shore. You can also arrange for someone to pick you up about five and a half miles farther north at the

Alpine Boat Basin.) We caution walkers not to bring small children on this outing; between the river and the sheer cliffs, they will be hard to watch and protect.

The shore path is narrow, sandy, occasionally rough with fallen rocks from the cliffs to your left, but always passable. The narrow beach, with its rocks and huge boulders strewn about, is immediately on your right—so close, you can often step into the water. The walk is mostly shady, a great place on a hot day with its gentle river breezes; it is brilliant with foliage in fall, but icy in winter. There are only occasional white markers, but as you follow the river's edge, you cannot get lost. As you go north, you'll find a stretch that was once a settlement of small farms, quarries, and fishing shacks before the park was created. You'll also see the remains of a cemetery along the river in one of the few meadow areas, as well as occasional docks and rocky lookout points. There are vines and tall grasses, honeysuckle and berries, and all kinds of thick vegetation in spring and summer, and many, many birds. Here and there you'll come upon a stone picnic table—created, of course, from fallen boulders. After about three miles you'll find the picturesque Greenbrook Falls, in a beautifully wooded setting. The next two miles are slightly more difficult, with stone steps here and there, and a few washouts where the river has risen over the beach. At the boat basins at either end of the walk you'll find rest rooms, snack bars, and parking, in season.

Both parks are open year-round. Fee for parking in season. Telephone: 201-768-1360.

❁ If you prefer to walk way above the river, atop the Palisades, where the views are spectacular and the going is slightly easier, take the **Top of the Palisades Walk.** Six sets of stairs connect this path with the road below. Trails are marked. Caution: Although some areas are fenced, there are many dangerous cliffs just below you along this walk. Remember that you are at the top of mighty rock faces, so do not hover near the edges! We do not advise bringing small children on this walk.

❁ **Flat Rock Brook Nature Center,** on the other hand, is ideal for a family outing, children in tow. This very pretty nature center on the western slope of the Palisades is not only a good walking spot, but also provides all kinds of environmental and educational programs at the Nature Center building. You will seldom find as active a nature center, nor as nice a set of family-oriented trails—more than three miles of them. There is a path covered with tulip and sweet gum leaves, as well as streams, ponds, volcanic rock formations, quarry cliffs, wetlands, and meadows. A walk—or many walks—here will introduce you to one of the region's most interesting geological and natural areas. We particularly liked the boardwalk around a former quarry going into the woods and meadows, which allows access to strollers and wheelchairs, and is suitable for people who simply like to walk on dry wood walkways. Remember to pick up printed guides to the trails, and to the many birds to see, at the center before you go off on your walk.

A part of the Nature Center, but perhaps a separate walk, is the nearby Allison Park on Jones Road. (You can hike here from the Nature Center, too.) Here, just beyond the pleasant, woodsy picnic grounds, where you can cook out near the swings and meadow with gurgling brook, is a surprisingly nice, gentle climb into the woods. This is at most a 25-minute walk but it is always delightful. It was once the wooded property of a private estate, lucky enough to have its own lake, waterfall, and tumbling brook. The trail (marked by white blazes) climbs—with steps and paths—always upward alongside the downhill stream. (Bigger kids will love this safe place to play on boulders in the shallow brook on a spring or summer day.) Though you are literally only minutes from the George Washington Bridge, you will feel wonderfully woodsy and cut off from the city here. As you climb, always keeping the brook on your left, you'll come to a small lake and a waterfall. Ducks and other waterfowl have also discovered this spot. We recommend this walk at any time of year—even in winter, though watch out for ice.

Open year-round. Telephone: 201-567-1265.

Overpeck Park presents a different aspect of the Palisades area. All the way down at the bottom of the western edge of the cliffs is the Hackensack riverbed, providing an entirely different ambience. But it is nonetheless quite beautiful with its marshy terrain, great waving reeds, and terrific bird watching. Though much of the park is devoted to various sports and recreational areas, you'll find a trail going south from the (left-hand) entrance deep into the reeds. Take it! This is one of those odd experiences where the grasses are probably taller than you are, and you walk among them listening for birdcalls and spotting various waterfowl and other birds as well.

Open year-round. Telephone: 201-944-3249.

 IN THE VICINITY
Tenafly Nature Center
The Tenafly Nature Center is another recommended site in this Palisade region, for it too is on the western side of the Palisades and has a similarly interesting terrain (though fewer boulders!). Featuring about a mile and a half of marked trails, it is a pleasant, not too difficult hike that passes a picturesque little lake. (Ice skating here in winter).

Open year-round. Telephone: 201-568-6093.

4·
PATERSON
REGION

The Great Falls, Paterson.

Romantic Vistas: The Great Falls,
Castle Ruins, and Mountain Trails

♨ HOW TO GET THERE

Paterson Great Falls

From Route 80, take exit 57B to "Downtown Paterson." Turn left onto Cianci Street, left again onto Market Street. Make a right onto Spruce Street, go one block to McBride Avenue Exit. The Visitor Center is on the right corner.

Lambert Castle

From Route 80, take exit 57 to Route 19, Clifton. Take first exit at Valley Road. Turn right at top of ramp and follow signs.

Garrett Mountain Reservation

Enter at Lambert Castle, or continue south on Valley Road to main entrance.

Only 15 miles from Manhattan, this area is a surprise to many of us who might not imagine the grandeur of this great waterfall or the wilderness of Garrett Mountain so close to the urban scene. The opportunity for a day away from urban and suburban sprawl so near at hand is extraordinary—given the surrounding population density. And these are not mere parks, but wonderful, romantic spots to visit.

🦋 **Paterson Great Falls** is one of the natural wonders of New Jersey, not to mention the entire region. Some 15,000 years old, the chasm through which these falls roar and tumble was created by an earthquake 200 million years ago. They are thought to average two billion gallons of water a day! These great falls have been likened to Niagara Falls, and in fact, they do make you marvel at their height and power. So too did Alexander Hamilton when he saw them in the late 1700s and imagined Paterson as an industrial center whose mills would be powered by the 77-foot high, roaring falls.

Along with Pierre Charles L'Enfant (the designer of Washington, D.C.), Hamilton conceived of a system of elevated raceways that would carry water and produce energy from the Passaic River. His plan worked, and Paterson became a center of industry—the first planned industrial city in the nation. By the end of the nineteenth century, the city had 300 silk mills and was known as the "Silk City of the World." (Today you can still see the vast network of old brick mills from times past—most now unfortunately empty—and in fact, you can tour the entire historic district.)

As many times as we have visited them and walked above them—for that is what you can do here—we are overwhelmed by the beauty of these falls. Leave your car in the parking lot opposite the Visitor Center, pick up a self-guided walking tour there, and walk up the hill on Spruce Street toward the Hydroelectric Station. (Built between 1913–14, it is one of the earliest in the nation.) Enter the falls area via the path behind this large brick building. Here in what is known as Mary Ellen Kramer Park (for the woman who fought to preserve this wonderful spot), you'll find a pleasant path with a spectacular view from a bridge directly above the tumbling waters. The roar here, particularly after heavy rainfall, can be deafening. You'll love it! You can also walk down to various levels below via stone steps. Watch your children carefully here!

You can continue your explorations by taking a series of rather run-down paths through the falls area; they eventually lead down to the river level where there might be a fisherman seated on a glacier rock in the midst of the swirling waters. And across Spruce Street from the hydro-electric plant is the Gatehouse, circa 1846, and the canal system that travels among the mills. If you like early engineering and waterways (the first canal here was constructed in 1792), this will interest you, as you can see the complex system with its three tiers of canals and their spillways.

The falls can be visited in daylight hours; the Visitor Center is open from 9 A.M. to 4 P.M. weekdays, and from May 1 to October 30 on weekends, too, from noon to 4 P.M. Closed on holidays. Visiting is recommended just after heavy rainfall for optimum thundering. We also recommend that you visit this rather isolated spot in broad daylight when other walkers and tourists are around, or call to join a group taking the guided tour. There is no admission fee. Telephone: 973-279-9587.

Lambert Castle was the showplace home of one of the silk magnates whose mills in Paterson were powered by the Great Falls. Catholina Lambert was an Englishman who came to the United States in 1851 at the age of 17 to make his fortune. And he succeeded: by 1890 he was one of the largest mill owners in Paterson. He built his "castle" on Garrett Mountain (see below) to house himself and his family as well as a growing collection of fine art and antiquities. (You can visit the castle—it is operated by the Passaic County Historical Society—and see some of his collection, though much of it was lost in an economic depression in 1916.)

Of particular interest to the walker will be the surroundings of Lambert's big stone castle overlooking the urban scene below. Lambert chose a setting that is quite wonderful: his house is built on very hilly terrain, which rises to a real plateau, and atop the mountain sits what appears to be an ancient ruin. If you leave your car near the mansion, you will find a fine but very steep path that takes you to the top. (You can also drive there via the entrance to Garrett Mountain Reservation.) The views are terrific, and once there, you'll find a ruin every bit as romantic as the remains of a walled European castle. (Apparently it was once Lambert's observatory.) There are decaying stone walls, a tower, old windows, and giant rocks, and what a vista! (Children will love this spot and the hikes around it.)

Lambert Castle is open Wednesdays through Sundays from 1 P.M. to 4 P.M., year-round, but the grounds are open daily from dawn to dusk. There is a small charge for the castle, but the grounds and parking are free. Telephone: 973-881-2761.

Garrett Mountain Reservation is the very large area (575 acres) of which Lambert Castle is merely a tiny corner. This reservation is surprisingly rustic and unusually hilly in the generally flat terrain of eastern New Jersey. It is heavily wooded, filled with rock faces that reminded us of the Palisades area of the Hudson Valley, and it is wonderfully off the beaten track. Although there are stables here and fishing in several pretty ponds and lakes, it is primarily an undeveloped area. We saw a few hikers who probably couldn't believe that they could be so remote yet so close to home!

Mounted policemen patrol the area, and there are both car roads (be careful, they are all one-way) and footpaths and many great lookouts to the sprawl below. Roadways, footpaths, and bridle paths circle through the reservation and run around its perimeter, so be sure to get a map before you set out. Almost all of this reservation is hilly; do not attempt it if you only like flat terrain.

Garrett Mountain Reservation is open dawn to dusk daily, year-round. There is no entrance fee. Telephone: 973-881-4832.

5·
MONTCLAIR
REGION

*Nature
Tended
and Wild:
Cherry
Trees, a
Picturesque
Cemetery,
Formal
Gardens,
and a
Nature
Preserve*

Cherry blossoms at Branch Brook Park.

⚱ HOW TO GET THERE

Branch Brook Park (Belleville)

From Garden State Parkway, take exit 149 to Belleville Avenue (east), and follow signs to the park. (You will enter on Mill Street.)

Bloomfield Cemetery (Bloomfield and Glen Ridge)

Take exit 151 from Garden State Parkway to Watchung Avenue (going west), left onto Broad Street, and continue for several blocks; right on Belleville Avenue for about one block. The cemetery is on your right.

Van Vleck Gardens (21 Van Vleck Street, Montclair)

From the Garden State Parkway, take exit 148 (Bloomfield Avenue, west); continue on Bloomfield for about 2.5 miles. In Montclair, turn right at Valley Road; go through traffic light at Claremont Avenue, and take the next left (Van Vleck Street). The gardens are immediately on your left.

Mills Reservation (Reservoir Drive, Cedar Grove)

From the Garden State Parkway, take exit 151 (Watchung Avenue), go west on Watchung Avenue for about two miles until you reach Upper Montclair Avenue. Go north for about 1.7 miles and make a left onto Normal Avenue. The reservation is less than a mile away, on your left.

Essex County has its share of urban and suburban congestion; it also has quite a number of wonderful green spaces, from groomed gardens to rustic parklands. Below are some we have particularly enjoyed in the Montclair region.

❀ If you think that Washington, D.C., has the largest concentration of flowering cherry trees outside of Japan, think again! That honor falls to **Branch Brook Park**, right here in New Jersey. (We, too, were surprised by this unexpected discovery.) In fact, the claim is that this long, narrow 486-acre park has the largest such collection in the world. And, if that weren't enough to lure you to these parts (particularly at cherry blossom time in mid to late April), you may also be surprised to learn that Branch Brook was designed by John Charles Olmsted, stepson of the master landscape designer Frederick Law Olmsted, in 1900, and that it is considered to be the oldest county park in the nation.

This vast park can be seen by car or on foot. Since it covers quite a large area, you may first wish to drive through, to get a general sense of where to go. For walkers there are pleasant footpaths that meander among the flowering trees, over small bridges, and along a stream. There are almost 3,000 trees, representing more distinctive cherry varieties than we ever realized existed. In April they appear as delicate clouds of white, muted red, and pink, sending forth the most seductive fragrances.

A recommended two-mile walk begins at the Visitor Center, turning left at the playing fields onto a paved pathway. When you cross the stream you are in the heart of cherry blossom fairyland. You can continue walking on looping paths over and around the stream, enjoying spring daffodils and forsythia scattered about in random beds. You can turn back at Broadway, retracing your steps, or make your own route.

Branch Brook Park is open daily, year-round, dawn to dusk. During cherry blossom season (mid to late April) there are many visitors; if you prefer solitude, come on a weekday. There is no entrance fee. For more information call 973-621-7199.

🌺 Cemeteries can be unusually nice places for walking and enjoying nature. Most are necessarily quiet and peaceful sites, and some are beautifully planted and carefully groomed. Others contain historic graves or artistic mausoleums. **Bloomfield Cemetery** is an interesting combination of all these elements, making it well worth a visit.

This picturesque cemetery is set on five acres of gently sloping terrain, behind an iron gate with large stone pillars. Much like an arboretum, it is filled with graceful flowering trees and shrubs. We saw dogwoods, cherries, beeches, and many azaleas. And, because no artificial flowers are ever allowed on the grounds (as a sign proclaims), the ambience is truly naturalistic and uncommercial.

This is also a historic cemetery, with quite a number of old sandstone markers, some even dating from the eighteenth century. In fact, the brochure you can pick up at the office (located in a lovely stone building at the entrance) will give you the names of the most illustrious people buried here. These range from members of prominent families in the region, to state politicians (New Jersey governor John Franklin Cort, for one), composers (Charles Griffes is among them), artists (Charles Warren Eaton, a Hudson River painter), noted university professors, successful business people, and many more. Although the cemetery does not include true "mausoleums" with winged angels or the like, it does have beautiful old graves that harmonize with the peaceful surroundings (and are intriguing to decipher, too).

The cemetery is open daily, from 8 A.M. to 5 P.M. (the office closes at 4 P.M.). There is no entrance fee.

✿ **Van Vleck Gardens**, tucked away on a leafy street in Upper Montclair, are one of the better kept garden secrets around. Immaculately tended and formal—though not stiffly so—and at the same time romantic, they are in every way inviting.

The gardens are picturesquely set on five acres surrounding an elegant Italianate house. From the 1870s until the 1990s (when it was opened to the public), this was the estate of the prominent Van Vleck family, some of whom evidently were passionate gardeners. The site includes a small group of gardens, some magically hidden behind towering hemlocks, as well as expanses of lawn, shaded walkways, trellises, pergolas, and magnificent plant specimens. Some of the many rhododendrons bear the names of Van Vleck family members.

Before beginning your leisurely stroll through the grounds, pick up a garden map at the entrance. One of the highlights is undoubtedly a pair of majestic Chinese wisterias that adorn the courtyard next to the house. These not-to-be-believed beauties (dripping with enormous and intensely fragrant lavender blossoms) have apparently been clinging to their supporting stone pillars for some sixty years. The plants and stone are so intertwined that they have virtually become symbiotic. (We observed an artist busy at work, trying to capture the remarkable scene on paper.)

The courtyard faces the elegant formal garden. In the center is a sweeping lawn surrounded with azaleas, dogwoods, mountain laurel, and rhododendrons, among other varieties. Here, too, is an impressive cedar of Lebanon.

The Azalea Walk is a particular treat in spring, when it becomes a raucous festival of oranges, pinks, reds, and whites. The Rear Garden is another delight, with its specimen trees and flowering shrubs, a large dawn redwood, blue Atlas cedar, star magnolia, Scotch pine, Chinese holly, and the ubiquitous azaleas and rhododendrons (these were clearly among the Van Vlecks' favorites, judging by their numbers).

Keep wandering and you'll find Mother's Garden, home to Japanese wisteria, flowering dogwoods, and mountain silverbells; the Carriage House Garden, where such unusual varieties as Arizona cypress and Japanese scholar tree can be found (not to mention more azaleas and rhododendrons); and the Drying Yard, profuse with Japanese yew. There is a greenhouse, too, where Howard Van Vleck—the last of the family to live here before his death in 1992—hybridized yellow rhododendrons, among other varieties. Some of his original plants still grace the property.

Van Vleck Gardens are open daily from 1 P.M. to 5 P.M., May through October (but remember that the specimen wisteria and rhododendrons are best in spring). There is no entrance fee. Telephone: 973-744-0837.

 For a complete change of ambience we take you to the nearby **Mills Reservation.** The gently hilly, woodsy site is a rustic and untended spot, where nature is basically left to its own devices. These 157 acres include the Lenape Trail and three miles of marked footpaths with an overlook.

In this quiet place you are alone with your natural surroundings. You'll find few (if any) people and no concessions at all. We recommend Mills Reservation to those who simply enjoy a walk in the woods, with no frills. Come in spring, fall, or winter; summer can be buggy!

Mills Reservation is open dawn to dusk. There is no entrance fee. For more information call 973-857-8530.

IN THE VICINITY
Presby Memorial Iris Garden

If you have a passion for iris (and many do, judging by the numbers of visitors who come here during late May and early June each year), this two-acre garden is a must. There are more than 70,000 plants representing 6,000 varieties (most are examples of the so-called tall bearded iris variety), making this possibly the largest iris collection in the country. Neatly set in long rows at the base of a gentle hill, the plants are carefully identified with metal markers. Look for the blue-white Florentina iris dating from the 1500s, Japanese iris (these bloom from mid-June to July), and the nineteenth-century "Honorabile," among others.

Presby Gardens, named after the late Frank H. Presby, founder of the American Iris Society, were laid out in 1927. Today they are carefully maintained by the local volunteer organizations. Open daily, dawn to dusk. Best time to visit is late May and early June, although some iris bloom later in the season. No entrance fee. The garden is located at 474 Upper Mountain Avenue, Upper Montclair. Telephone: 973-783-5974.

6·
LIBERTY
STATE PARK

Liberty State Park with New York City skyline.

The Great City Skyline:
Scenic Walks on the Hudson's
Jersey Side

֍ HOW TO GET THERE

Liberty State Park

Take exit 14B on the New Jersey Turnpike and follow signs to the park. There are several different walks within this state park: Green Park, Liberty Walk, and the Nature Path.

If you want to take an out-of-towner for a walk, you might consider this park; it has perhaps the most spectacular vistas of any park in the world! The saving of this great piece of Hudson River shoreline for a park is surely one of the smartest and most successful enterprises of the last decades. The most jaded viewer will ooh and aah at the sight of Manhattan, Ellis Island, and the Statue of Liberty so close by, silhouetted glamorously before you with every step you take. (Before the tragedy of September 11, 2001, the Twin Towers of the World Trade Center were central to this panoramic vista; walking here today will also give you a bird's eye view of the site and its ongoing development.) The flat terrain of this shoreline, both the natural tidal marsh and the lovely plantings, the boardwalks and walkways, and the old buildings of this one-time transportation hub make a walk here quite perfect—and that's even without visiting Miss Liberty or the great Ellis Island so nearby.

֍ **Liberty State Park** has had a notable history, since it borders New York Harbor and is only a short ferry ride from the big city. The first ferry from here sailed in 1661. The Morris Canal once terminated here, and loads of coal and other goods arrived at this spot. The great era of rail travel and commerce is very much in evidence; you can walk in the huge echoing train terminal (a beautiful 1889 red brick edifice) and see where the numerous tracks converge. Ellis Island, where so many of our ancestors arrived to become Americans, is just beyond; it was here that some eight million immigrants boarded trains that took them to their new destinations. The sense of history is palpable. You can't help imagining the arriving strangers seeing the Statue of Liberty in the harbor, making their way through the great halls of Ellis Island, taking a ferry to this shoreline and starting out from this very spot toward their new lives.

In 1976 the park was dedicated as New Jersey's Bicentennial gift to the nation. Today it is extremely popular with tourists from all over the world. It is here that they can get ferries to the Statue of Liberty and Ellis Island, as well as a water taxi to Manhattan and tour boats around New York. There are numerous interesting displays and events and a large marina, but just walking on the paths described below will be an undoubted thrill. For the least crowded times go during the week, and arrive in the morning. And take your kids!

If you are driving, you might begin your outing by visiting the Interpretive Center (in a notable building designed by Michael Graves), to pick up information and a good map. For the first walk described below, we recommend that you park near the playground. For Liberty Walk, park as near as you can to the great Rail Terminal; if you prefer to walk north on Liberty Walk, drive to the end of Freedom Way, where you can also leave your car. For the nature walk, park near the Interpretive Center.

Green Park is a very large (88-acre), recently planted, quite flat park that lies behind the riverfront area, between the Interpretive Center and the Rail Terminal. It is prettily landscaped (though the trees are not yet very large), and has wonderful vistas throughout; you'll see the torch of the Statue of Liberty, for example, as you rest on a bench, or the Empire State Building, as you meander through these agreeable acres. There is a nice playground for the kids, as well as a beautiful picnic area.

Liberty Walk is the pièce-de-résistance of the park, however. This two-mile walkway is one of the great walks in the entire state. The spectacular views of Manhattan, New York Harbor, Ellis Island, and the Statue of Liberty, the Staten Island Ferry, and even the famed Brooklyn Bridge make this vista seem cinematic; you can hardly believe you are looking at the real thing! The close proximity of the city to this shoreline and the fact that the walkway is directly above the waterfront allows you to view everything unimpeded, except perhaps by an occasional fisherman. Few people seem to take this long, straight walk, so you can do so with great freedom from crowds. (Most people are lined up waiting for the ferries to take them to the Statue of Liberty and Ellis Island.) Liberty Walk, which we have enjoyed many times, is part of the Hudson River Waterfront Walkway, which will eventually allow you to stroll all the way from Bayonne to the George Washington Bridge.

You can begin Liberty Walk at its starting point (at the mouth of the Morris Canal near the marina, just beyond the North Overlook) or at the terminal (walk by the front of the rail building in the direction of Ellis

Island). You will end up at the Liberation Monument at the South Overlook and the United States Flag Plaza. Conversely, you can begin at the south end and walk all the way to the terminal, thus having the view of New York City ahead of you the whole time.

The land that forms Liberty Park was originally a tidal marsh, mainly a salt marsh that formed part of the Hudson River estuary. You can see evidence of the natural growth of marsh plants (and many birds) in the areas that are adjacent to the park. Fortunately, some of the natural tidal marsh has been left in its original state and forms part of the park. The Nature Path takes you through one such area. If you start out at the Interpretive Center, you'll see signs to the Nature Path. Here, complete with wildlife viewing observation points, you can walk through the burgeoning reeds and grasses that dot the marsh and circle a small pond. Sixty acres are included in the natural area. Not far away are sites for fishing and crabbing. With its juxtaposition of natural and urban views, this is a fascinating walk.

In addition to these three interesting walks, you may also want to visit the nearby marina. Many visitors combine a walk at Liberty State Park with a visit to the Liberty Science Center, one of the preeminent children's science and technology museums.

Liberty State Park is open from dawn to dusk daily. There is no fee for visiting it (or Ellis Island or the Statue of Liberty). There is a fee for the ferries and for parking. Telephone: 201-915-3400.

 **IN THE VICINITY**

Weehawken

Another inspiring view of Manhattan from the Jersey side can be had all along the river in the city of Weehawken, a few towns north of Jersey City and Liberty State Park. A nice green walk of a couple of miles has been laid out here; it overlooks the river and the view and also has its own interest. It is precisely along this shore that Alexander Hamilton and Aaron Burr fought their duel.

7·
GREAT SWAMP REGION

Wildlife Walks: Songbirds, Owls, Butterflies, and Waterfowl

The Great Swamp.

⚓ HOW TO GET THERE

Lord Stirling Park and the Great Swamp
National Wildlife Refuge

Take Route 80 west to Route 287 south; take exit 30A onto North Maple Avenue (south), turn left at Lord Stirling Road. Follow signs for both Lord Stirling Park (which comes first) and the Great Swamp.

Scherman-Hoffman Sanctuaries

From Route 287, take exit 30B and turn right onto North Maple Avenue; go through traffic light at the Old Mill Inn, onto Childs Road, then bear right onto Hardscrabble Road. Follow signs to the New Jersey Audubon Center (Scherman-Hoffman Sanctuaries).

The Great Swamp and its surrounding region are among New Jersey's greenest and most pristine areas, with vast expanses of unspoiled and protected marshland, ponds, and forests. The swamp is what remains of an enormous (10 by 30-mile) glacial lake that was formed during the Ice Age. Not surprisingly, this relatively untouched area provides an ideal habitat for wildlife, from waterfowl and birds of all kinds to fish and other varieties. If you are a birder and naturalist you won't want to miss the sites described below.

Lord Stirling Park and the Great Swamp National Wildlife Refuge are both within the Great Swamp Basin; the former, an 897-acre county park, is situated on its western edge, adjacent to the refuge, a vast 7,450-acre protected area run by the U.S. Department of the Interior.

The Great Swamp originated about 25,000 years ago, after a massive glacial lake known as Glacial Lake Passaic disappeared, leaving behind extensive swamps and marshes, one of which was the Great Swamp. During the eighteenth century the Delaware Indians deeded some 30,000 acres of these wetlands to English investors. Small farms and settlements were soon established, but the difficult terrain made them uneconomical, and most failed. The area was destined to become the site of an international airport in the late 1950s. Fortunately, a band of local citizens and other concerned conservationists joined forces, raised funds, and donated the land to the government for public use, guaranteeing that it would remain forever wild.

Lord Stirling Park and the Great Swamp National Wildlife Refuge are ideal environments in which to view birds and other wildlife. The terrain is mostly flat and includes swamp woodland, hardwood ridges, marsh, grassland, brush, ponds, and pastures. More than 200 species of birds, as well as a surprisingly large variety of mammals, reptiles, and amphibians, can be seen. There are blinds and observation sites for viewing. (Motorized traffic is forbidden in certain sections and severely restricted in others.) Birding and nature watching at the much smaller Lord Stirling Park is an easier proposition, with readily accessible trails starting right next to a large parking area; the trails within the Great Swamp National Wildlife Refuge are more remote, which may make them appealing to those seeking a challenge. Both facilities conduct nature tours—including occasional owl prowls, marsh meanders, and other wilderness adventures. Both also offer a wide variety of educational workshops and discussions on relevant subjects.

🐾 **Lord Stirling Park** offers more than eight miles of walking trails with observation towers and blinds. An extensive waterside boardwalk gives visitors—including those in wheelchairs and even small children—access to the many species of waterfowl and plants found here. Before setting forth, you should stop at the Environmental Education Center to pick up a trail map and brochure describing all the things to see. (This large and well-equipped 1977 building was apparently the first solar-heated and cooled structure in the country.) Here, too, you'll find a permanent exhibit describing the swamp from prehistoric times to the present, with some 15 displays.

What is now Lord Stirling Park was, in colonial times, a part of the very vast estate of one William Alexander, Lord of Stirling, a general in the Continental Army. His Georgian mansion is open to the public one day each year, in connection with an October festival celebrating colonial New Jersey.

We especially recommend a wonderful 3.5-mile trail (including the boardwalk mentioned above), which starts along the banks of Branta Pond, an artificially created lake. In addition to the sometimes raucous ducks and geese that enliven this water scene, you might spot muskrats. In spring and summer you can enjoy small trailside herb gardens that stand out in contrast to the surrounding natural flora. If you follow the red markers, the path will lead you to wet forests of beech, hickory, and oak; a freshwater swamp, home to a rich variety of flora and fauna; and fields dotted with wildflowers and butterflies in summer. From various lookouts you might observe eastern kingbirds, meadowlarks, field sparrows, and other species of songbirds.

The park is open every day, year-round, from dawn to dusk; the building is open from 9 A.M. to 5 P.M., except holidays. (Summer hours are extended.) Telephone: 908-766-2489.

🐾 Just a couple of miles away, off Lord Stirling Road, is the entrance to the **Great Swamp National Wildlife Refuge.** The refuge is divided into two large sections. The western half, a wildlife management area, is intensely monitored to maintain the optimal conditions for wildlife; it has limited access to the general public, though it does include the refuge headquarters, a boardwalk, a wildlife observation center, and other amenities. The eastern half, the true wilderness area, includes about eight miles of hiking and walking trails.

You'll want to start your exploration of this vast site at the refuge office, where maps and extensive lists of wildlife are available, then head to the wildlife observation center, an ideal spot for viewing and photographing wildlife. From the nearby boardwalk (a shorter version of the one at Lord Stirling Park), you cross a marsh where you can see frogs, snapping turtles, and all sorts of birds.

Some endangered species have been spotted in the refuge. If you're lucky, you might catch sight of a bog turtle, blue-spotted salamander, or even a bald eagle. Bear in mind that the best times to see wildlife— whether it be birds, foxes, raccoons, muskrats, or what have you—are in the early morning and late afternoon. To observe waterfowl and other waterbirds, come in early spring during migration times. And remember to wear sturdy shoes or boots, as the trails can be soggy in places. During the summer months it might be a good idea to bring insect repellent to ward off mosquitoes and ticks.

The refuge office is located on Pleasant Plains Road and is open from 8 A.M. to 4:30 P.M. on weekdays. During spring and fall it may be open on Sundays, too. There is no admission fee. Telephone: 973-425-1222.

🐾 For a different kind of nature experience visit the nearby **Scherman-Hoffman Sanctuaries**, a hilly and woodsy site operated by the New Jersey Audubon Society. Here, amid 260 acres of rolling countryside with dogwood trees and waving grass, you'll delight in hillside trails through woods and fields and along streams, whether or not you are a birder (more than

125 species of land and waterbirds have been sighted). In a peaceful setting with a minimum of signs or other intrusions, this is an ideal spot for anyone seeking a day away from the usual bustle of modern life.

The twin sanctuaries bear the names of the families who donated these lands to the Audubon Society over a period of time, starting in the 1960s. The Hoffman section provides a typically highland environment for native birds, while the adjacent Scherman section includes the lower-lying riverside habitat. (Each has a parking lot and center housing offices, a book store, indoor programs, information, and maps.) The walking is hilly in places and can be somewhat strenuous, but there are rewarding vistas to enjoy everywhere—and great variety in flora and fauna, too. Among the birds to look for are migrating land birds in the spring (robins, warblers, bluebirds); in fall you'll see tufted titmice, chickadees, cardinals, even red-tailed hawks and turkey vultures, among other varieties.

There are several nice hiking trails within the sanctuaries. One, the Dogwood Trail, makes a loop through a fairyland of dogwoods. It is, of course, best seen in springtime when the enchanting trees are in full bloom and migrant birds are arriving. A more ambitious (in terms of length, anyway) trail is the Patriot's Path, part of which is still being developed. When completed it will include some 20—mostly riverside—miles for bikers, hikers, equestrians, connecting a number of historic sites, open spaces, and parks. But, for our purposes, we recommend a reduced version, with great natural beauty and historic interest, too. (Trail maps at either center indicate the best route.) It was in these parts that the New Jersey Brigade of George Washington's army camped during the winter of 1779–80, probably because of the iron ore and forge found here. The section of Patriot's Path that we recommend meanders along the Passaic River (here, surprisingly pristine), following occasionally steep, woodsy terrain, and eventually joining the Dogwood Trail on the way back. Note that there are well-marked detours here and there, leading to such places as Jockey Hollow or the Cross Estate (a charming Victorian garden well worth taking the extra time to visit).

Hiking trails are open daily until 5 P.M., year-round; the centers are open Tuesday to Saturday, from 9 A.M. to 5 P.M., and Sunday, noon to 5 P.M. There is no fee. Telephone: 908-204-8998.

8·
MILLBURN REGION

Winter along the Rahway River.

*Hawk Watching in a Wooded Reservation,
Walking in an Arboretum, and
Deep Woods with a Forgotten Village*

🪷 HOW TO GET THERE

South Mountain Reservation

From exit 14 of the New Jersey Turnpike, take Route 78 to Main Street, Millburn exit (Route 527). Go north to Brookside Drive and follow signs to entrance. (For the lookout described below, take the entrance on the opposite side of the park, from Millburn Avenue.)

Cora Hartshorn Arboretum and Bird Sanctuary

Although the entrance is very near the reservation, the easiest way to reach the arboretum is from Route 24 (exit 48 from Route 78 as above). Turn onto Hobart Avenue (right) and go right again at Forest Drive. The arboretum is at 324 Forest Drive South in Short Hills.

Watchung Reservation

From Route 78, take exit 44 and turn left onto Glenside Avenue. After 1.2 miles turn right into the reservation (Route 645). The road will take you past Lake Surprise and eventually to a parking area and the Trailside Museum. Pick up a trail guide at the parking area.

🐝 In this very crowded eastern area of the state it is wonderful to find several such serene spots to walk in. These three sites are unusually inviting to birdwatchers and wildflower enthusiasts in late spring through early fall. We were intrigued by the unexpected rough terrain of **South Mountain Reservation**—a very large (2,047 acres), very craggy area of woods and rock faces and glamorous vistas. (It is part of the Watchung Mountains—after the Leni-Lenape Indian words "Wach Unks" or "high hills.") As you can tell when you look out over a vast sea of development from this reservation, the saving of such a wild and lovely area of the state was a blessing.

The park has a 500-animal zoo, ice skating, picnic grounds, and various other amenities, but our particular pleasures were its wonderful walking trails—19 miles of them. Here, hawk watchers come to see graceful birds swoop off the rock faces. South Mountain Reservation is essentially a huge rock plateau with wooded hillsides. Tall beeches and oak trees abound. (Many were planted just over 100 years ago to refurbish a forest denuded by loggers.) Cross-country skiers have 20 miles of trails here. There are waterfalls, pond, and freshwater springs among the unspoiled woods and rocky crags. (We met a fellow who had been filling his bottles with drinking water from a spring there for over fifty years.) Leave your car at the parking area and follow the trails toward the hawk-watching area. You'll find the woods unmaintained—in a nice way—with many downed trees and somewhat rough and stony paths; wear good walking shoes for this one.

You can follow the trails all the way to the top of the mountain. The great lookout over the state (eastward) is from the opposite side of the park (you might prefer to drive up, as it is quite a climb, but don't miss it). On this side of the reservation you'll find Turtle Rock and a series of trails that skirt the edge of a great ravine. A trail map for the reservation is essential.

The grounds of South Mountain Reservation are open from dawn to dusk, year-round. The facilities, like the zoo, are open March through October. Grounds are free. Telephone: 973-857-8530.

A visit to the **Cora Hartshorn Arboretum and Bird Sanctuary** is a more intimate proposition. This very pretty preserve of just over 16 acres was created in 1924 by Cora Hartshorn, whose father was the founder of Short Hills. The site was bequeathed to the township in 1958. Wildflower gardens, maintained by local gardening enthusiasts, are a pleasure here, as are numerous rhododendrons, dogwoods, shadbushes, azaleas, and laurels. Specimen trees, including hollies and evergreens, dot over three miles of trails up and down this hilly terrain. And what is described as "an astonishing array of birds" frequents this pretty site; Mrs. Hartshorn counted 78 species.

Numerous programs having to do with ecology, birding, and trees take place on site and in the charming stone house headquarters. This is a very good place to introduce children to the joys of hiking in the woods, for many of the trails are short and there is plenty to discover.

The arboretum grounds are open daily, year-round. The stone house is open October to May, Monday through Saturday, from 9 A.M. to 3 P.M. (Saturdays only in the morning). Telephone: 973-376-3587.

Watchung Reservation covers over 2,000 acres. You will get an idea of how large this parcel of wooded mountains and lakes is by driving around it—it seems to go on forever. Like the South Mountain Reservation, this preserved land covers a very mountainous area overlooking the flat (highly developed) landscape to its east. George Washington used this high ground as a natural fortification against British troops, and you can still see why. This is a marvelous tract of almost pristine woods, with paths for horseback riding and hiking crisscrossing throughout. You'll find unusually tall trees here.

The longest trail through the reservation is known as the Sierra Trail (identified by white "blazes" or painted markers on the trees); it is some 10 miles long and will take you up and down and through the woods with terrific vistas, stands of hemlocks and redwood pines, brooks, and rocks. Shorter trails are also marked here, including one that skirts parts of the long and narrow Lake Surprise.

A particular point of interest at Watchung Reservation is the abandoned village of Feltsville. We were surprised to find this handful of still habitable-looking houses tucked away in the woods. One David Felt, a paper manufacturer (known as "the king" by his employees) insisted that everyone who worked for him live on site. Here, deep in the heart of the woods, are their homes, dating between 1845 and 1860. But after the mill closed, Feltsville became the more attractively named Glenside Park and was reincarnated as a Victorian retreat, with spring water, lawn tennis, and perhaps a magnesium spring as well. The tiny resort functioned until about 1916. Although the discarded houses and roads are today in disrepair, it is fun to imagine the village's past. (The state has promised to preserve the village.) Not far away is a cemetery for the Wilcox family, the original settlers from before the Revolutionary War.

We recommend that you pick up a trail guide at the Trailside Nature Center before setting out in any direction. (The Nature Center is at the intersection of New Providence Road and Coles Avenue.) It is not easy to find the various areas in this reservation, though some of them are accessible by car. But if you want to walk at the lake or see the deserted village, you will do best to read the map and drive to the nearest area for parking before setting out. Depending on your interests—in seeing the wonderful stands of oaks and pines, or walking along the Blue Brook trail (great for kids), or visiting the village—you will need to be clear about your destination.

Watchung Reservation grounds are open year-round, dawn to dusk. Telephone: 908-527-4900.

🎋 IN THE VICINITY
Rahway River Park

This is truly a riverside park, accessible from St. Georges Avenue, Rahway, where you can hike (or jog) along a pleasant flat path just next to the Rahway River with its pretty waterfowl and foliage. You can follow the river's rambling course through the area on an unusually pleasant path that is paved and ideal for joggers or for pushing strollers or wheelchairs.

9·
BERNARDSVILLE REGION

Cross Estate Gardens.

*Walking through Four Inviting Gardens:
Walled Victoriana, Hillside Rock
Gardens, a Naturalistic Delight,
and a Willowy Arboretum*

✦ HOW TO GET THERE

Cross Estate Gardens

From Route 287, take exit 30B to Route 202 north. Go left on Tempe Wick Road past the entrance to Jockey Hollow. Turn left onto Leddell Road at waterfall. Go 1.1 mile farther. Cross Estate Gardens is on Old Jockey Hollow Road in Bernardsville; make a left-hand turn onto the long driveway.

Leonard J. Buck Garden

From Route 287, take exit 22 to Far Hills. At the train station, turn right before the tracks, onto Liberty Corner/Far Hills Road. Continue for about one mile, and turn right on Layton Road to number 11, on your left.

Bamboo Brook Gardens

From Route 287, take exit 22 to Route 206 north. Go four miles to Pottersville Road (County Route 512). Go west on Pottersville Road and follow signs to the gardens and to Willowwood Arboretum, both of which are on Longview Road in Gladstone, Chester Township.

Willowwood Arboretum

Follow same directions as for Bamboo Brook Gardens. The arboretum is just down the road from the gardens.

New Jersey is called the Garden State with good reason, for some of the loveliest gardens in the East are to be found here. With a long tradition of cultivating crops and flowers, the state has every sort of garden—from the classical, more formal to the wilder rambling style. The area around Bernardsville has three of the most inviting public gardens to visit—particularly in late spring.

✿ **Cross Estate Gardens**, part of a historic area of Morristown's National Historic Park, are on a lovely estate that was laid out as a summer retreat in 1905. The gardens have an intimate charm that is thoroughly Victorian, with high walls and a profusion of blooms. Surrounding the formal flowerbed area is a charming landscape to walk through. You will feel as if you were wandering through an English turn-of-the-century estate.

A well-known landscape designer named Clarence Fowler designed the gardens, but Julia Newbold Cross, who purchased the estate with her husband in 1929, was apparently the guiding inspiration for the walled, English-style flower garden. (She was a long-time president of the New

York Horticultural Society.) The flower garden—now maintained by a group of dedicated volunteers—has been returned to its former glory after a long period of neglect. Geometric brick paths cross through ornamental beds, creating a wonderful arrangement of colors and textures and sizes. There is an enchanting, old-fashioned feeling to this intimate space, with its brickwork, cast-iron urns, and English ivy amid the day lilies, periwinkles, and coral bells.

The flower garden is the centerpiece of the estate. Around it you'll find a landscape inviting you to walk through it. Here a mountain laurel allée, there a fern-planted shade garden, a vine-covered pergola; shrubs and trees and blossoms wherever you wander. If your taste in walking is for a beautifully designed and maintained garden spot, the Cross Estate is certainly not to be missed. Open daily from dawn to dusk in garden season. Admission is free. Telephone: 973-543-4030.

Leonard J. Buck Garden is a completely different—but equally delightful—garden walk to enjoy. Here, the naturalistic garden surrounds, and includes, extraordinary rocky outcroppings in its design. Set amid some of New Jersey's loveliest rolling countryside, this garden is vast and hilly and has its own spectacular gorge. A pleasure to explore, the 33-acre garden is surrounded by glacial ponds and giant rocks; though it seems to be a wilderness, it is actually a carefully designed and nurtured environment.

Considered one of the premier rock gardens in the nation, the Leonard J. Buck Garden was laid out in the 1930s by Mr. Buck, a mining engineer who was fascinated by the great volcanic outcroppings on his property, and by a landscape architect named Zenon Schreibner. They used the extraordinary geological formations as the basis for a grand rock garden design. (These are not small garden-sized rocks, by the way!) An early ecologist, Buck was interested in the symbiotic relationship among plants, rocks, and soil, and he wanted to make his garden look as though it had been created entirely by nature. To this end, grand rock formations were unearthed from loose trap rock and soil, and exotic and woodland plantings were placed everywhere around them, filling the valley with rare plants as well as indigenous ones. Nature—in the form of wildflowers and shrubbery—has added to the original design. Walkways take you from one extraordinary spot to the next.

You'll find a walk here (or a guided tour, if you prefer) amidst the woodland flowers exceptionally beautiful and interesting. Among the delights are wild orchids and lady's slippers, viburnum and white violets, and mosses and ferns. (A pamphlet with trail guide is available at the entrance; if you want to see particular flowers in bloom, telephone in advance.) This garden's combination of the wild and the cultivated is irresistible. Each of the 13 massive rock formations has its own name and distinctive plantings—and each area is accessible by nice pathways, but has lots of ups and downs. (Wear sturdy shoes for this one.)

The garden is open from 10 A.M. to 4 P.M. Monday through Saturday; noon to 4 P.M. on Sunday in winter and 5 P.M. in summer. A small donation is requested. Telephone: 908-234-2677.

Bamboo Brook Gardens are unusually appealing. Having seen dozens of formally laid-out gardens, we found these so delightfully naturalistic and attractive in design and plantings that we recommend visiting at any time of year—even if everything is not in bloom. The layout, with its circular fieldstone walls, steps up and down, and small waterways and pools, is enchanting. But in spring, add the glorious blooming shrubs and flowers, and a bright sunshine dappling through tall trees and you have a garden to remember.

The approximately 100 acres include fields and brooks and forest and naturalistic plantings that allow for a good long walk filled with wonderful vistas. Or you can just meander among the well-arranged spaces that surround the house and the smaller buildings on the estate with an eye to garden design and the delicate geometric planning of paths and flowerbeds. Martha Brookes Hutcheson (the second woman in America to receive a degree in landscape architecture) laid out the gardens herself. By 1935 the five acres nearest the house had become a gracious semiformal garden. In following years, as trees matured into towering specimens (yellow-wood, cedar, white birch, hemlock, and sweet gum, among many others) and the stone walls aged, the gardens became increasingly attractive. You'll find both formal plantings and some two dozen different types of wildflowers as you wander around this picturesque setting. Throughout the estate there are watercourses, small reflecting pools, and the sounds of a gurgling brook.

In 1974 Mrs. Hutcheson's daughter donated the property to the Morris County Parks Commission. You can visit it daily, from 9 A.M. to dusk. There is no charge. Telephone: 973-326-7600.

Willowwood Arboretum offers yet a different style of garden very near Bamboo Brook. This 130-acre landscape was once a working farm, and the atmosphere of informality and relaxation makes it a great place for a hike amid flowers and dozens and dozens of trees, particularly—as you might guess—willow trees. In fact, there are over 100 types of willows growing here, and you can imagine how lovely they are in springtime.

Willowwood began as a farm in the 1700s and continued that way until 1908, when its owners, brothers Henry and Robert Tubbs, began to grow distinctive plants and trees in addition to vegetables (still being produced in neat rows). There are formal gardens here, too, including a Japanese-style pool garden and a cottage garden. But the true pleasures for the walker are the farm paths skirting the eighteenth-century residence and old barns, over a pretty stream (via a Japanese bridge), through wildflower fields, and into the marvelous collection of green and flowering trees.

You'll find many Asian touches here, including a Katsura tree, Japanese primrose, and groupings of bamboo. There are also magnolias, tulip trees, bald cypress, cherries, lilacs, and hollies—in all some 3,500 species of native and exotic plantings.

If you enjoy arboretums, this is certainly a walk not to be missed. It is also a very good place to take children; there is much to see in an informal and spacious setting. (Various educational programs are also offered here.) A descriptive trail guide is available at the entrance, or you can wander around as you like.

Willowwood is open daily, from 9 A.M. to 4 P.M., year-round. Admission is free. Telephone: 973-326-7600.

10·
MORRISTOWN
REGION

Delbarton School Garden.

*Patriot's
Path:
Great Hikes
through
Morristown's
Historic
Woods and
Lakelands*

 HOW TO GET THERE

Morristown National Historic Park:
Jockey Hollow Encampment and Patriot's Path

From Route 287 (south from Route 80), take exit 30B and head north on Route 202 about two miles to Tempe Wick Road; turn left. Entrance to the park is 1.5 miles farther, on your right.

Speedwell Village

Entrance to this section of Patriot's Path is on Route 202, just north of downtown Morristown.

Sunrise Lake, Louis Morris County Park

Entrance to this section of Patriot's Path is on Route 24—Mendham Road—a continuation of Washington Road in Morristown. Parking on west side of Route 24.

Loantaka Brook Reservation

Take exit 31 from Route 287 toward Madison. Entrance is on Spring Valley Road, southeast of Morristown.

Morristown, as most New Jerseyites know, is the historic center of George Washington's military endeavors and the site of the first National Historic Park in the nation. Here, amid the rolling hills and valleys of central New Jersey, are historic sites of encampments and the very trails and pathways taken by the Continental Army during the winter of 1779–80. Known as Patriot's Path, these more than 27 miles of trailway cover a large part of the national and adjacent county park, as well as continuing into the town of Morristown itself. The many parts of Patriot's Path within the National Historic Park include sections of varying length—ranging from a mile-long trail with red blazes (or painted markers on the trees) to the 6.5-mile white-blazed one. There is also a section of the trail that cuts through farmland and across roadways from Speedwell Lake north of Morristown to Sunrise Lake in the Louis Morris County Park. This is a series of outings that may provide you with many days of hiking, for this is an area of our state whose inhabitants early understood the importance of saving nature for generations to come.

Jockey Hollow Encampment is indeed the site of Washington's winter encampment, when cold, mutiny, smallpox, and starvation failed to defeat the determined Continental Army. Billeted here (you can still see several of the little cabins) with some protection from the nearby Watchung Mountains, these 10,000 men overcame desertion and every sort of privation to rebuild their army and emerge to defeat General Howe's Redcoats.

Begin your hike by picking up a trail guide at headquarters near the parking area, and choose the section of Patriot's Path you wish. As you can see from the map, the sections overlap and intersect and are well marked. The hiking is not difficult and paths seem filled with historic import. (The government has wisely kept intrusive signs and gimcrackery out.) The immensity of this park (1,675 acres) and the untouched quality of much of the woodland give one a good idea of Revolutionary War New Jersey. (If you visit in winter, you'll also have some feeling for the cold and misery that the soldiers endured.) You can walk in this site at any time of year from 9 A.M. to sunset (Visitor Center is open until 5 P.M.) There is a small fee. Telephone: 973-543-4030.

Another section of the historic **Patriot's Path** was actually used as a rail line long after its Revolutionary War days. In 1888 the Rockaway Valley Railroad Company (known familiarly as the "Rock-a-Bye Baby" Railroad) built a 25-mile line from White House, New Jersey, to just north of Morristown at Speedwell Lake, where stagecoaches met the train and ferried passengers and goods into downtown. Its major source of revenue was peaches—bushels of them; on one day in 1896, some 72 cars of peaches left the area. In 1917 the line was discontinued after enduring economic woes. The line's terminus was at Speedwell Avenue, where we find the path today.

At the beginning of this section of the path you'll see a lovely dam and some ruins. No, they are not from Revolutionary times, but the remains of a nineteenth-century iron factory, where the first telegraph was built. Just across the road you'll find historic **Speedwell Village,** a re-creation of a town from 1800. The path wends its way along the lakeside—several huge white swans were there when we visited—and on through the countryside and suburbs, and across the road a time or two. After some five miles it will take you to the Whippany River and eventually to its end at Louis Morris County Park.

You can also enter the same five-mile walk from the south (as noted above). You'll find several more miles of hiking trails in this county park's

1,154 acres of deciduous woodlands and other park amenities, including swimming at **Sunrise Lake.** This walk is less bucolic than those within the National Park, but it is interesting in its own way, with its small bridges, grade crossings, and changing scenery. Telephone the Morris County Park Commission for information: 973-326-7600.

Loantaka Brook Reservation is a large county park that has been left in an attractively pristine state. It offers bridle and cross-country trails, ice skating, and eight miles of pathways—equally divided between paved and unpaved. We recommend it for biking and skiing in particular, though walking through its 574 acres is also very pleasant. A nice combination of fields and woods, with a lake in the center, Loantaka Brook Reservation is quiet—no traffic sounds! The park is open from dawn to dusk and there is no charge. Call the Morris County Park Commission for information: 973-326-7600.

IN THE VICINITY

Along with the Revolutionary War Patriot's Path, Morristown offers numerous other historic sites to visit. You will find a brochure describing such interesting sites as Washington's Headquarters and Wick House at the Visitors' Center at Jockey Hollow Encampment. Among the others are the following:

Traction Line Recreational Trail

Traction Line Recreational Trail was once a Morris County trolley track taking people from the Morristown Railroad Station to the village of Madison. Known as the Traction Line, it has now been converted to a walkway that runs alongside today's railroad line. Although it skirts some unsightly industrial buildings, it does run through a golf course and two college campuses, and all is not lost! You can do a series of bone-crunching exercises en route during this five-mile hike: there are exercise stations all along the way. Pick up a guide at the Convent Railroad Station at the south end, or at the Morristown Station. Telephone the Morris County Park Commission for information: 973-326-7600. (Be careful where you leave your car; spaces are clearly marked at the station yard.)

Frelinghuysen Arboretum

Frelinghuysen Arboretum consists of over one hundred acres of gardens, distinctive trees and shrubs, in addition to all kinds of horticultural wonders. This is a bustling place, divided into a variety of botanical units. There are a number of walks within forests and meadows, and pretty perennial beds and flowering shrubs. If you prefer manicured nature to the wild, you'll enjoy the shade garden, the winter garden, a fantasy pond, and other specialty areas. There is a garden for the disabled, and gardens that are designed for therapy. The arboretum is located at 53 Hanover Avenue in Morristown. Open daily 8 A.M. to sunset, year-round; closed major holidays. Telephone: 973-326-7600.

Delbarton Gardens

Delbarton Gardens is a 400-acre campus and the setting for the Delbarton School, a Catholic prep school, about three miles west of Morristown. Its grounds are open to the public, and its formal Italianate gardens are worth a visit. Here, in the most unlikely of settings—a former Benedictine monastery—are Roman columns, both standing and artistically ruined and lying on the ground. A great columned pergola is banked with numerous ancient statues of Roman gods and warriors, with an occasional winged angel. The plantings are lovely, and the campus itself is spacious and inviting. Delbarton School is on Mendham Road (also Route 24) in Morristown. The campus is open weekdays, from 9 A.M. to 5 P.M., weekends 9 A.M. to dusk. Free admission. Telephone: 973-538-3231.

11·
MOUNTAIN
LAKES
AND BOONTON
REGION

*Images of
Impressionism:
A Reflective
Lakeside
Walk,
Carpets of
Wildflowers,
and a
Sun-Dappled
Wooded
Landscape*

Wildflower walk in Tourne County Park.

🌿 HOW TO GET THERE

Birchwood Lake (Mountain Lakes)

From Route 46 at Mountain Lakes, turn right on The Boulevard to Pocono Road, then right on West Shore Road to the end, where you'll see a sign for the Richard M. Wilcox Memorial Park. The lake is located within the park.

Emilie K. Hammond Wildflower Trail (Tourne County Park)

From Route 46 at Mountain Lakes, take The Boulevard all the way to a fork in the road; bear left onto Powerville Road. Take the first road on the left, McCaffrey Lane, and follow signs for the park.

Old Troy Park (Parsippany-Troy Hills)

From Route 46 in Parsippany, turn left onto S. Beverwyck Road. After about one mile the road splits, and you bear right onto Reynolds Avenue for another mile. You'll see the park entrance on your left.

Morris County is endowed with some of New Jersey's loveliest natural wonders, from picturesque lakes and luminous vistas, to dreamy woodlands and hillside views. The walks described below are set within such landscapes and are evocative of impressionist images, with their subtle tableaux, delicate colors, and filtered light. (They might be a case of nature imitating art!) In a sense, you might think of the following as "artwalks" as much as "nature walks."

🌸 **Birchwood Lake** is located in a public park on the end of a quiet street in Mountain Lakes, a tony and idyllic community of abundant greenery, gentle hills, and clear lakes. Because the site is popular with swimmers in the summer (note that only local residents can swim here, although out-of-town visitors are always welcome to enjoy the park's walking trails), we recommend an off-season visit, when its quiet and reflective ambience can be enjoyed at its best.

Leave your car at the park entrance and follow a gravel path that winds around and above the lake and through the woods. This loop is approximately one mile in length, with romantic water views at every turn. Look through the trees and you can see the peaceful lake with its delicate lily pads and soft reflections of clouds and trees, so reminiscent of Monet paintings. When the light is just right, this is a truly poetic moment.

If time is not a problem, you can also explore some of the park's woodsier trails, accessible from various points along the lakeside loop. (These are well marked.)

The park is open daily, from dawn to late at night (11 P.M.), year-round. There is no fee for walking. Telephone: 973-326-7600.

Just a few miles away in Boonton is Tourne County Park and its enchanting **Emilie K. Hammond Wildflower Trail.** This ruggedly beautiful 545-acre park of forests and hills and huge granite boulders takes its unusual name, "Tourne," from a Dutch word meaning "lookout" or "mountain." Indeed, its highest point affords spectacularly panoramic views of New York City's skyline.

The Tourne is one of New Jersey's gems, with more than 200 shrubs and wildflowers, myriad species of native ferns, and dense woods of white oaks, beeches, maples, and hemlocks. The park is apparently the only remaining undeveloped fragment of the Great Boonton Tract, which was purchased in colonial times by David Ogden, then colonial attorney-general of the state. McCaffrey Lane, its main access road, was then the route for hauling iron ore to the Ogden ironworks nearby. (Cannon balls were made in the Boonton region during the Revolutionary War.) The park itself was created through the efforts of the civic-minded Clarence Addington DeCamp, regarded as the first conservationist of Morris County. Over the course of his lifetime (1859–1948), he inherited and acquired the parkland and laboriously, with hand tools and levers, built two roads to the top of the Tourne for public enjoyment.

One of the park's main attractions is undoubtedly the wildflower trail, most easily reached by entering the park via Powerville Road. This woodland garden is a "must-see" particularly in springtime, when it becomes a magical carpet of colors and shapes and the dappled light will remind you of a Renoir. Named after a local botanist who created the trail in 1961 and identified its many flowers, it features a mile of interconnecting, narrow paths winding through different terrains that can accommodate the surprising number of plant varieties. In this relatively contained area you'll find low, boggy spots and high, dry areas; sunny slopes and deeply shaded glens; and a gurgling brook creating the loveliest of background sounds.

A self-guiding leaflet listing all plants and bloom times is available at the trail entrance. (The flowers are also identified on site.) Alongside the first stretch you'll find such varieties as purple violets, bluebells, and Dutchman's breeches. A right fork leads to the Brookside Trail and its wetlands filled with skunk cabbage; nearby are wild orchids, too, as well as the delicate pink lady's slipper. In spring the Swamp Trail is a mass of cardinal flowers, lilies, buttercups, and marsh marigolds; the Fern Walk Trail features the expected profusions of ferns, but the surprise comes in their many varieties (some 25, we are told). The Trillium Walk may be the highlight, with its spectacular spring displays of every version of this flower, from toad trillium, to snow trillium, to the tiny dwarf white trillium.

The Hammond Wildflower Trail is also home to some magnificent trees, including a remarkable beech tree that dominates a wooded area. Across the way from the trail you'll see signs for a bird sanctuary (the Eleanor Hinrichsen Memorial Bird Sanctuary), where you can spot the likes of the white-crowned sparrow, white-breasted nuthatch, purple finch, dark-eyed junko, and saw-whet owl.

Before leaving Tourne Park altogether and if you're feeling energetic, you might wish to undertake the Decamp Trail, a rugged uphill woodsy hike that leads to "Top of the Tourne"; at this 897-foot-elevation lookout point you are rewarded with memorable Manhattan views. Another not-to-be-missed site is a 54-ton boulder called the Mouse Cradle Balancing Rock. This glacial phenomenon is balanced on two points of ledge rock and a hidden wedge stone; when DeCamp discovered a mouse nest in a cleft of the rock in 1897, he adjusted the boulder to save it.

Tourne County Park is open daily, from 8 A.M. to dusk. There is no entrance fee. Telephone: 973-326-7600.

🐾 The nearby **Old Troy Park** is, in fact, not so old at all. First opened to the public in 1978, it includes some 96 acres of lovely woodland, grassy fields, swampland, and a charming pond. This is a quiet park, perfect for families with children, with its playing field, creative play equipment, picnic sites, horseshoe courts, and pleasant walking trails. The terrain is flat or, at most, gently sloping.

What we especially enjoyed in this genuine and uncommercial place was a woodsy path that took us through some lovely impressionistic vistas. We walked inside a silent, cleared forest of tall, vertical trees, with no underbrush other than carpets of delicate groundcover. The combination of the dark, almost black, trees and the tiny dots of soft green plants underneath, along with the sunlight filtering through reminded us of a scene from a Seurat painting. The path leads to an idyllic pond, complete with yellow-blossomed water lilies and the reflections of overhead clouds. We encountered no one, save for one lone fisherman by the pond.

There are other walking trails, as well (pick up a park brochure at the entrance), which in winter are also used for cross-country skiing and snow-shoeing.

Old Troy Park is open daily from dawn to dusk. There is no charge. Telephone: 973-326-7600.

IN THE VICINITY

Pyramid Mountain Natural Historical Area

This 1,000-acre wilderness offers rugged hiking trails, forests, fields, cliffs, swamps, and amazing rocky outcroppings. On this ancient land giant boulders were deposited by the so-called Wisconsin Glacier some 18,000 years ago. You can see two of these massive wonders from the Blue Trail and the White Trail (two of the park's five hiking trails): Tripod Rock, an enormous boulder balanced on three smaller rocky outcroppings; and below it, Bear Rock (ten times as big!), one of the largest such glacial erratics in all of New Jersey. For thousands of years this land was hunted and fished by the Lenape Indians. In fact, some scholars claim that Tripod Rock was part of an ancient calendar site used by Native Americans for summer solstice observations.

The Blue Trail, one of the most popular (it leads to Tripod Rock and scenic lookouts), is quite arduous and steep and strewn with boulders. Unfortunately, the walk includes a stretch beneath power lines and high voltage towers, perhaps not as picturesque a setting as one might like. An alternative is the Yellow Trail, which is very woodsy and peaceful.

Pyramid Mountain is also a wildlife sanctuary and home to many birds and mammals (including bears and bobcats). Hundreds of different native plant and wildflower species thrive in this mountainous terrain. Look for woodlilies, cardinal flowers, witch hazel, viburnum, and many, many ferns.

This area is located on Boonton Avenue, Montville Township. For guided trail walks call the Visitor Center. The park is open daily, dawn to dusk. There is no entrance fee. Telephone: 973-334-3130.

12·
FROM JENNY JUMP
TO SPARTA

Waterloo Village.

Rural New Jersey: Mountains,
a Ghost Lake, a Scenic Rail Trail,
and a Historic Village

HOW TO GET THERE

Jenny Jump State Forest

There are two entrances to this section of Jenny Jump State Forest. Take exit 12 off Route 80 to Route 521 south. At the light in Hope turn left on Shiloh Road (Route 519); you'll find one entrance is on your right. For another entrance, take Route 611 from Hope and follow signs to entrance, which is off Shades of Death Road. Both entrances will take you to the trail to Ghost Lake.

Sparta Mountain

The town of Sparta is north of Route 80; take exit 34 to Route 15. At Sparta's center take Route 620 east to Edison Road. The trail's entrance is marked by a kiosk on Edison Road.

Sussex Branch Rail Trail

From Route 80, take exit 25 to Route 206 north. After a little over a mile go left on Route 604 (Waterloo Road). Go one mile toward Allamuchy State Park, and leave your car at parking area directly opposite Continental Drive. Entrance to the Rail Trail is marked.

Waterloo Village

From Route 80, take exit 25, and follow signs.

This area of New Jersey is unusually hilly—even mountainous—and pleasantly rural. Here veteran hikers, mushroom hunters, bird watchers, and other nature enthusiasts who don't want to travel terribly far from their own urban areas can find a variety of scenic places to walk near Route 80.

Jenny Jump State Forest is actually made up of two separate areas in a wonderfully wild and quite unpopulated area. This walk is in the more northern of the two, but there are trails in both sections. In the part nearest the highway, there are two particularly nice, panoramic trails that lead up and down through the wooded hills and their spectacular boulders, and all the way to a lovely body of water called Ghost Lake. There are also good biking trails within the forest. We recommend picking up a map, with trails and scenic lookouts noted, at the entrances before you set out.

Jenny Jump may get its name from a legendary—or mythical—story related by a Swedish missionary named Sven Roseen in 1747. He reported that a colonial woman named Jenny was gathering berries with her father when Leni-Lenape Indians approached, and the father advised her to jump off the ridge. This perhaps apocryphal story is countered by another, suggesting that Jenny Jump is simply a version of the native name for a lovely, hilly spot.

In order to access the Ghost Lake Trail, you have two options. If you park at the first entrance as noted above you can take the Summit Trail (1.5 miles) to the Ghost Lake Trail (1.3 miles), through lovely woods and boulders. If you park at the second entrance, you will find yourself at the lake in minutes, and can take the Ghost Lake Trail as far as you like away from the water. All of the trails in Jenny Jump are somewhat hilly and rocky, but anyone who likes nonflat hiking should be comfortable on them—with proper shoes.

You can also visit the observatory at one of the highest spots in the forest. An astronomical site called Greenwood Observatory was opened at this scenic spot in 1995; it has the largest equatorial mounted telescope in the state. On Saturday evenings from April through October you'll find it open for viewing.

For information on Jenny Jump State Forest and the observatory, call 908-459-4366.

Sparta Mountain is quite different in terrain from Jenny Jump. This is a wetland forest containing what the Audubon Society describes as "one of the finest and least disturbed glacial basin swamps in the state." Needless to say, the birds like it too. Many threatened and endangered species live on Sparta Mountain, including no less that 22 types of warblers, and black bears, bobcats, and other wildlife. Only recently saved from development, this area owes its preservation to local citizens groups and organizations; it is one of 30 permanently protected regions in the state that are administered by the Audubon Society.

Some 349 acres of wetland bogs adjoin 1,400 acres of preserved land with its own network of marked trails. You'll have your choice of highland and wetland trails to explore. This area is particularly recommended for wildlife and bird-watching enthusiasts.

Pick up a map before you go! For information call the New Jersey Audubon Society at 908-204-8998.

The Sussex Branch Rail Trail is a delightful trail, just the right width—excessively flat and easy to hike, and beautifully set. In fact, you will not want to turn around and go home on this one, even though it runs for almost 15 miles, from an entrance in Allamuchy State Park at Byram all the way to Lafayette, north of Sparta. The passing scene ranges from burbling brooks way below the walkway to isolated lakes (like Jefferson Lake, once a source for cutting ice, with an Ice House siding that still stands), to people's backyards, to ruins of old construction, to the wonderful "Hole in the Wall," a bridge built in 1853. This is a particularly picturesque rail trail.

Built in the mid-nineteenth century, the rail line was originally designed to provide access to iron ore in the town of Andover, one of the villages on this route. The major mine was only seven miles from the port of Waterloo (see below) on the Morris Canal, and originally a narrow-gauge rail line was to run from Andover to Waterloo, with the ore then being carried by barge to the Delaware River. It opened in 1851. By 1864 the line had been extended, and the Sussex Railroad went on to become a coveted property, acquired in the 1880s by the Lackawanna, becoming the Delaware, Lackawanna and Western Railroad. Time ran out for the rural little line about 100 years later, and today we have the long and interesting hiking trail available to us. (By the way, you can also access this rail line hike at the towns of Andover, Newton, Hampton, and Lafayette.)

🌺 Although well known as a National Historic Site and the site of a fine music festival, **Waterloo Village** is not so familiar to walkers. But its antique buildings and setting on the Morris Canal and the Musconetcong River and Waterloo Lake make it a marvelously picturesque place to walk. Waterloo is a preserved community with homesteads, blacksmiths, taverns, general stores, a nice canal house, and a sawmill—among the thirty-odd structures on its winding lanes. For the walker who is tired of nature walks, they offer all sorts of interesting sights and diversions and a real feel of history. Take the kids on this one!

Waterloo has a distinctive history, beginning with a Leni-Lenape village on the site, and subsequently involving Revolutionary-era forges and water-driven industry. In 1778 the Loyalist-owned Andover iron industry was confiscated by the Americans, and Waterloo became a source of pig iron and then steel. By 1831, with the opening of the Morris Canal, the village became an important port, with its own stagecoach inn, school, and canal house, as well as a number of other buildings.

After you've walked through the village on your self-guided tour (get a nice map and descriptions at the gate), you can begin your walk along the waterways, crossing over the little bridges and intersections of the three bodies of water that border the village. There is even a picturesque waterfall.

The village is, of course, quite a school-trip attraction, and you are best off visiting on the weekends. Waterloo is open (at a somewhat steep fee) from early spring through November. Telephone: 973-347-0900.

13·
THE NORTHWEST
CORNER OF
SUSSEX COUNTY

High Point State Park.

New Jersey High Points:
A Ravine, a Waterfall,
a Mountain Trail, and a Lake

🖉 HOW TO GET THERE

Tillman Ravine (Stokes State Forest)

From Route 80, go north on Route 206 to Branchville. The Stokes State Forest office is five miles north; for the ravine, go west of the office and south on Strubble Drive. (Tillman Ravine is marked and is about three miles from Route 206.)

Buttermilk Falls (Stokes State Forest)

From Walpack Center within the forest, go south on Mountain Road for about three miles. The falls are on your left.

High Point State Park (Monument Trail)

From Route 80, take Route 23 north to the town of Sussex. About eight miles north of town you'll find High Point State Park on your right (though the headquarters are on the left side of Route 23); follow signs to the trail.

Swartswood State Park

From Route 80, go north on Route 206 to Newton. From the center of town, go down the hill, turn left on Mill Street (Route 622), and left again at Swartswood Road.

New Jersey's scenic highlands in its northwest corner combine vast parklands with great panoramic vistas. Pristine lakes, waterfalls, dense forests, and only a few towns here and there are part of the landscape; in remote wooded areas, you might even come across an occasional bear or two.

🌿 Not surprisingly, this green, unspoiled region provides great hiking and walking opportunities. In the most rugged spots—for example, in the Kittatinny Mountain Ridge within the vast Stokes State Forest—are various rigorously challenging trails that link to the Appalachian Trail; we leave those to the most committed of hikers. Following, instead, are pleasurable walks that we especially enjoyed for their beautiful natural settings.

Situated within the 15,000-acre Stokes State Forest, **Tillman Ravine** is an enchanted woodland of towering trees and dramatic rocky formations surrounding a brook cascading down a sharp incline. Geologically speaking, the steep and narrow (and therefore young) ravine was created by melting glaciers some 10,000 years ago. Today it is a magical tableau of red shale outcroppings and deep green hemlocks and pines, accompanied by the melodious sounds of rapidly moving water, rustling branches, and many birds.

This peaceful 375-acre site is a delight at any time of the year—from the hottest of summer days (when its moist microclimate can make it surprisingly refreshing) to cold winter spells (when oddly shaped ice sculptures might form along the stream). In spring there are masses of wildflowers, not to mention brilliantly colorful rhododendrons, azaleas, and dogwoods. It's a great spot for anyone to explore, including families with children.

You can create your own path down the ravine (it's impossible to get lost if you simply use the stream as your guide) or follow a marked mile-long loop. In either case, your starting point is just a few feet down from the parking area, where you are enveloped at once by the beauty of your surroundings. You'll be amazed at the height of the graceful hemlocks—some soaring up to the sky at least 100 feet. The forest is also rich with oaks, maples, black birch, hickory, sycamores, and flowering dogwoods.

If you walk down the slope along the water, you come to the first of several little wooden bridges, where you can pause for a moment to view the falls and cross the brook. Toward the bottom of the ravine is a favorite spot known as "the teacup." Shaped like a large bowl with smooth walls, it was created by sand and rock particles swirling in the rapidly moving water. Though swimming is unfortunately not permitted, you can certainly put your feet in the water to cool off—as many people do on hot days.

The ravine is open daily, year-round, from dawn to dusk, without charge. (Note that on some snowy days the road to it may be closed.) Telephone: 973-948-3820.

Buttermilk Falls are just a few miles from the ravine, but in a more remote part of the forest. Having had a somewhat difficult time in locating the falls ourselves, we were not surprised to learn that few people knew of them in the first place. We had been driving for what seemed miles and miles (actually only three) on an unmarked and unpaved country road, past open fields—hardly where you would expect to find a waterfall—when, quite suddenly, woods and hills appeared, and then the sounds of rushing water.

Situated on a rugged hillside with tall trees and big red rocks, the spectacular falls are well worth the effort. Aside from their natural beauty, they are among New Jersey's highest falls, cascading gracefully down the Kittatinny Ridge for some 85 feet. (The other two falls with that distinction are Paterson's Great Falls and Bergen County's Greensbrook Falls.) To get their full dramatic impact you must climb up a fairly steep wooden walkway to the very top, where you'll find a viewing area.

Stokes State Forest is open year-round, dawn to dusk (see above), and Buttermilk Falls can be seen at any time of year. In winter, call first to make sure the access roads are open: 973-948-3820.

In the extreme northwest and highest point of New Jersey is the appropriately named **High Point State Park**, a 14,000-acre area of ridges, valleys, ancient rock formations, and magnificent panoramic views. Lying along the rugged Kittatinny Mountains, just north of Stokes State Forest, it is filled with rich plant life and wildlife—including bobcats, coyotes, fox, and bears (or so we've heard).

The park's most distinctive feature, however, is its historic High Point Monument, a 220-foot needle (vaguely reminiscent of the Washington Monument) that commemorates New Jersey's war veterans. At 1,803 feet this 1930s structure dominates the summit. If possible, climb to the top (as of this writing the monument was still under renovation) for an all encompassing view. You can see not only the nearby Delaware Water Gap, Kittatinny Ridge, and the Poconos, but also the distant Catskills. Monument Trail, a 3.5-mile loop, begins here, just off the monument's parking lot.

This trail is certainly among the most scenic of the ten or so in the park. Even though it can be rough going in places—with some fairly steep uphill sections—it is suited for most walkers, including willing children. The trail circles around a lovely glacial pond (Lake Marcia), through a ridge-top forest of hickories and oaks, into a ravine (where coyote footprints can sometimes be spotted in winter), and through more highlands and woods before coming back to the starting point.

Toward the end of the trail, in a valley below the final ascent, you'll see a sign indicating Cedar Swamp Trail, a 1.5-mile loop definitely worth a detour (or even its own, separate, walk.) If you follow those markers you'll find yourself in the picturesque Dryden Kuser Natural Area, New Jersey's first such designated site (dating from 1965). In addition to a vast bog (formed during the last ice age) and its surrounding ridge, the area includes a virgin woodland of hemlocks, black spruce, white pine, and less common southern white cedar. During cold winters much of the park's wildlife comes here, seeking protection from high winds.

High Point State Park, including all trails, is open from dawn to dusk, all year. Telephone: 973-875-4800.

 While the walks described above require some climbing, the trails in **Swartswood State Park**, a pleasant 1,400-acre park near Newton, in the Kittatinny Valley, are mostly easy and flat. Within the park are two lakes (used for swimming, boating, and fishing), streams, marshes, woods, and three nice walking trails. One, Duck Pond Trail, is actually paved, making it ideal for baby strollers and wheelchairs. (Bikers and skateboarders are also welcome.)

Duck Pond Trail begins near the park entrance, where you can pick up a map. This woodsy one-mile trail overlooks the pond most of the way. This is an out-and-back walk; you must either retrace your steps or connect with nearby Spring Lake Trail, a 2.8-mile loop that winds through woods before reaching a small lake. The Grist Mill Trail is the third—and steepest—walk. Named after one of the early mills that existed in the region from the time of the Revolutionary War, it is a 1.2-mile loop with great panoramic views of Swartswood Lake.

Swartswood State Park is open daily, year-round, from dawn to dusk. Telephone: 973-383-5230.

IN THE VICINITY
Peters Valley Craft Center

Situated in a remote wooded site within the Stokes State Forest and the Delaware Water Gap, Peters Valley is a genuine craft community of artists and artisans who live and work here, usually for a year's time. Fortunately, they are willing to share their world not only with students who come to learn about their art, but also with the more casual visitor who is interested in observing these works in progress. On summer weekends you can see artisans working in ceramics, fine metals, textiles, photography, and wood in small studios scattered about in the woods.

A walk through this rustic site is not only interesting for those who like crafts, but also a treat for nature lovers, for this is a spot of great beauty. As you wend your way from one studio to the next, you will discover many an inviting path through the woods and might be tempted to wander farther afield into the vast surrounding national park.

Before you start out, pick up a self-guided walking tour map available at the Peters Valley Craft Store (which, by the way, displays many of the works done on the premises). The charming frame house with an old-fashioned porch is directly in front of a most unusual Greek Revival–style house, which turns out to be the photography studio. Across the street is the Peters Valley office, where you can get all the information you need; and, on the floor above it, the Doremus Gallery, which features annual shows.

Peters Valley Craft Center is open every day, year-round, but studios are open only on summer weekends, from 2 P.M. to 5 P.M. Phone first to check exact schedules. It is located on Route 615, Layton. Telephone: 973-948-5200.

14·
WARREN
COUNTY

*Delaware
Water Gap:
Four
Samplings
of a
Spectacular
Region*

Worthington State Forest.

🔥 HOW TO GET THERE

Dunnfield Hollow Trail (Mt. Tammany)

Take Route 80 west all the way to the Delaware Water Gap. Take the last New Jersey exit road before crossing the Delaware River toll bridge and continue north for about three miles. Park at the rest area lot on the right, where the trails for Mount Tammany begin. (We recommend, however, that you first stop at the Kittatinny Point Visitor Center to get information, maps, brochures, etc. The Center is just beyond the rest area, on the east side of the road.)

Karamac Road Trail

Karamac Road Trail, less than a mile west of the Visitor Center, begins at the traffic signal on Old Mine Road, which runs parallel to the river.

Van Campens Glen (Worthington State Forest)

Continue north for approximately 10 miles on Old Mine Road (the river will be on your left). Follow signs for Van Campens Glen, leave your car at the parking lot, and look for the yellow-blazed Van Campens Trail into the woods.

Paulinskill Valley Trail

The trail starts near the town of Columbia on the Delaware River. From Route 80 west take exit 4 onto Route 94 north for one mile, then right onto Brugler Road. After crossing a little stone bridge, you'll find the trail head on your left.

The Delaware Water Gap is among the great natural wonders of the eastern United States. Its centerpiece is, of course, the majestic Delaware River, which winds, twists, and curves picturesquely through the Kittatinny Ridge (part of the Appalachian Mountains). Surrounding the river is a spectacular panorama of forest (Worthington State Forest), rocky crags, glacial lakes, mountain streams, and deep gorges.

It is not surprising that people have been drawn to this region for some time, from the early Leni-Lenape Indian settlers (who came for the abundant water supply and wildlife), to Dutch explorers to modern-day tourists. After the railroad penetrated the region in the 1850s, quite a number of visitors appeared, staying sometimes for months in large, comfortable resort hotels that have since vanished.

In 1965, the Delaware Water Gap National Recreation Area was created, with 70,000 acres set aside for public use. Visitors today can enjoy fishing, canoeing (understandably a very popular activity here), camping, exploring, and hiking. There are more than 60 miles of hiking/walking trails of various levels of difficulty and time commitment. Below are four samplings that we especially enjoyed: the first three are within the park itself, in close proximity to one another, while the fourth is just a few miles away. All these trails are unusually scenic, as you'll discover.

Before starting, we recommend you stop first at the Kittatinny Visitor Center for information, maps, and lists of wildlife to look for at any given time of the year.

Dunnfield Hollow Trail, within the Dunnfield Creek Natural Area in the southern edge of Worthington State Forest, is an absolute must for any hiker wishing to explore the region. Here is a lush array of stately hemlocks, sugar and striped maples, black birches, oaks, ashes, tree-sized rhododendrons, and enormous boulders. At the center is the creek, which tumbles over large rocks as it descends rapidly from Mt. Tammany to the Delaware River. Walking here is a treat at all times of the year. In the fall the brilliant leaves glisten in the sunlight, in spring the mountain laurels are abloom in pink and white splendor, and winter and summer bring their own natural pleasures. You can also spot various birds (some 40 species have been identified), foxes, and deer.

After you've left your car in the big, woodsy parking area off the road, look for the well-marked trail signs. Dunfield Hollow Trail, part of the vast Appalachian Trail (white blazes, or markings painted on the trees), was once a logging road. It climbs gently and gradually along the creek and is fairly broad and easy to negotiate, making it ideal for families with children (who find the large rocks and small waterfalls irresistible). At Holly Spring a red-blazed path veers off to the right, connecting with a green blaze. If you choose the shorter (two-mile) route, this is the time to circle back (turning right). Otherwise, you can continue for another two miles to the scenic Sunfish Pond, a beautiful glacial lake. You can also loop around the pond before turning back.

Another option is to follow the "red trail" up to Mount Tammany, also accessible from the same parking area. This is a much steeper, more challenging, but an equally popular hike, not recommended for young children. At the top is a truly magnificent lookout over the Delaware Water Gap, making the fairly arduous climb well worth the effort. As you sit and rest on the ridge you can look for hawks that occasionally swoop overhead.

Trails are open year-round, dawn to dusk. For further information, call the Kittatinny Point Visitor Center at 908-496-4458.

🌿 Nearby is **Karamac Road Trail**, providing a very different walking experience. Unlike Dunnfield Hollow Trail (or the steep trail up Mt. Tammany, for that matter), this is a mostly flat path that includes only a short climb at the end. In fact, the trail follows an old railroad bed along the Delaware and, as such, affords lovely river views.

The trail begins beyond a small parking area at the traffic signal on Old Mine Road, a road presumably built by early Dutch settlers to transport mining loads. At first you might be put off by the traffic sounds of nearby Route 80, but soon the winding river and path change direction, away from the noise. You walk through dense woods, overlooking the river on one side and hilly terrain on the other. You've reached the end when you come to a parking area. This is an out-and-back trail, just a little more than a mile each way.

Open daily, year-round, dawn to dusk. For more information, inquire at the Kittatinny Point Visitor Center.

🌿 To reach **Van Campens Glen** you continue driving on Old Mine Road for about 10 miles, along the river and through the woods until you reach a sign where you can leave your car. The magnificent views overlooking the winding Delaware with its picturesque little islands literally take your breath away.

Van Campens Glen (named after early Dutch settlers) is a magical, dark forest of tall hemlocks and beeches, steep rocky slopes, and a deep gorge. The only sounds you hear are those of birds and the brook that forms little cascades as it moves swiftly along.

The trail itself goes all the way to Millbrook Village (about five miles round-trip), a re-created nineteenth-century rural community that is no longer inhabited. But you can take an abbreviated route, simply by turning back at any point along the way.

The walk is quite steep and involves clambering over tree roots and moss-covered rocky ledges that can be slippery when damp (best not to take small children or to go when it's been raining). The path climbs and descends, crosses the brook on steppingstones (a challenge when the water is high), and continues up a steep rocky outcropping to the top of a dramatic waterfall—the upper Van Campens Falls. Stop for a moment at this unusually scenic spot and look down at the pool below, where occasional anglers can be seen fishing for trout.

Van Campens Glen is wonderful to explore at all times of year. Bear in mind that in summer, when its majestic hemlocks filter out the hot rays of the sun, the temperature here is quite a bit cooler and more pleasant than in surrounding areas. In summer you'll also find Millbrook Village bustling with volunteers demonstrating various crafts to visitors. (Its schoolhouse, gristmill, general store, etc. are open from late April until late October, Wednesday to Sunday; craft demonstrations on weekends only. No fee.) For additional information, contact the Kittatinny Visitor Center or Millbrook Village: 908-841-9531.

The Paulinskill Valley Trail, once a rail bed for the western portion of the New York, Susquehanna and Western Railroad, is a delicious, 26-mile greenway along the picturesque Paulinskill River, connecting Columbia in Warren County with Sparta Junction in Sussex. Most of the time you'll be walking near the river, as you make your way through lowland forests (maples, elms, sycamores), over little bridges, along a dam, and through open fields. Along the way you'll find a rich array of shrubs and trees (including the unusual Chinese ailanthus), banks of wildflowers (in spring), and ferns in great profusion. The wildlife here is also plentiful, and you might spot beavers, otters, muskrats, and deer. This is an easy, mostly flat, cinder path, ideal for walkers, joggers, bikers, horseback riders, cross-country skiers, children, even wheelchairs.

From the 1880s until mid-century, the railroad in this corner of western New Jersey transported coal, milk, wood, ice, farm produce, and other commodities, benefiting the various rural communities as it crossed from Pennsylvania to New York. (Along the trail you can still find historic artifacts from that era: remnants of ice houses, station foundations, railroad bridges, and such.) When the state first proposed converting the railbed into a parkland, there was opposition from politicians and property owners. Fortunately (for the public), the efforts of the local Paulinskill Valley Trail Committee paid off; Kittatinny Valley State Park was established in 1992 to preserve the trail and its surrounding land.

The Paulinskill Valley Trail is open from dawn to dusk daily, all year. Telephone: 973-786-6445.

15·
ALLAMUCHY
AND WEST

Red Trail, Merrill Creek Reservoir.

*Off the
Beaten Track
in Western
New Jersey:
Walking
across
a Dam,
through
Woodland
Preserves,
and Wildlife
Havens*

֍ HOW TO GET THERE

Merrill Creek Reservoir

From Route 80, take exit 12 (Route 521) heading south. Go one mile to Route 519, and continue on 519 south for 16 miles. Bear left at Y intersection of Routes 519 and 646. After 1.3 miles on Route 646, go left on Fox Farm Road to Richline Road, where you turn right. Continue to Merrill Creek Road; follow signs to Visitor Center.

Pequest Trout Hatchery and Wildlife Management Area

From Route 80, take exit 19 to Route 517 south to Hackettstown. At intersection go west on Route 46. Continue for nine miles. Entrance is on your left.

Allamuchy State Park, Deer Park Pond

From Route 80, take exit 19 and go south on Route 517 for about two miles. Go left on Deer Park Road to parking area.

Stephens State Park (adjacent to Allamuchy State Park)

Follow Route 517 as above, but turn off Route 517 turning left at Bilby Road. At intersection with Waterloo Road (Route 604) make a left to park entrance.

Warren County is one of the state's most naturally beautiful areas, and it is one which has been most able to avoid suburban sprawl. The forested hills (remember, we are not far from the scenic wonders of the Delaware Water Gap here) and pristine lakes are home to many beautifully preserved parklands. Wildlife likes this area, too. There are beaver dams, deer, many birds, including ospreys and bluebirds, fish galore, and even an occasional bear. When you hike around these areas you will find it hard to believe you are little more than one hour from the metropolis. These are fairly remote trails and should be undertaken with care and a companion.

֍ **Merrill Creek Reservoir** is certainly one of the most pristine and glamorous of destinations for the walker. Where else can one hike on the edge of a clear blue reservoir, and actually walk across the clear bright blue water atop one of its several long dams? The reservoir covers 650 acres, and the surrounding woodlands include 2,000 more. The entire preserve area is on a rise, a small mountain known as Scotts Mountain, and it is in an isolated area that is literally hidden away from major roads and tourists. The reservoir was constructed to store water for release to the Delaware River in times of drought, and to replace water used by seven electric utility companies, which have jointly opened the area to the public for hiking and fishing, boating, and cross-country skiing. (This is one of the few sites in our book that is privately owned, and it is a fine example of what industrial giants can do to preserve and open land to the public for walking.)

When you get to the Visitor Center, you'll find a good map, and several options of trails. There is a 290-acre wildlife preserve with a blind along the shoreline, in addition to trails that run directly to the water's edge or through the forests. Choose the trail you want (one features an abandoned orchard, another leads to a defunct lime kiln, and yet another takes you to the original creek); and note carefully the color of the blazes or painted markers you will follow, for this is an undeveloped area. Many of the trails are less than one mile long, but they are somewhat rough to walk upon. We particularly enjoyed hiking atop the dams and seeing the relief spillways and dikes. (If you choose the dam areas to walk in, you can park closer to that part of the Perimeter Trail, leaving your car at the Inlet/Outlet Tower on Fox Farm Road.) One of the most striking sights is the shoreline region of stark gray, dead trees rising out of the edges of the reservoir.

Merrill Creek Reservoir is located at 116G Montana Road in Washington, N.J. Trails are open dawn to dusk; the Visitor Center is open from 9 A.M. to 5 P.M. daily, except holidays. Telephone: 908-454-1213.

The Pequest Trout Hatchery and Wildlife Management Area is a one-of-a-kind experience, certainly for those of us who are unfamiliar with how all of those trout seem to be endlessly available in the brooks and streams and lakes of our state. Children will love this outing. The numbers of fish are startling. Here, some 600,000 brook, rainbow, and brown trout are raised, in order to be stocked in some 200 bodies of water. Set in 4,000 acres of a lovely Warren County landscape, the fish hatchery is just part of a great place to walk.

Begin your hike at the hatchery, where you can tour the facilities and learn all about the process, and feed some gorgeous trout swimming around at the front of the center. Then visit the most dramatic part: at the top of a small rise is more than a mile of concrete raceways, where thousands upon thousands of tiny fish go swimming by. (Four times a day, a truck releases fish food into the raceways; this is something to see!)

The natural area in which the trout hatchery is located was chosen for its clear streams: they supply some 7,000 gallons of pure water per minute. (The water is treated before being released back into the Pequest River.) When you leave the hatchery, pick up a trail map; you'll find there are three lovely trails, all recommended for children. Combining pond, forest, and farmland (with very very tall corn in season), there is much to see on these picturesque winding trails. This is an area that reminds you of "being in the country;" it is partly cultivated, partly wild, all beautiful.

The Pequest Fish Hatchery and Natural Resource Education Center is open from 10 A.M. to 4 P.M. daily, except holidays. The trails are open dawn to dusk, daily. For information contact the N.J. Division of Fish and Wildlife at 605 Pequest Road in Oxford. Telephone: 908-637-4125.

Neither of the above sites is wild, compared to **Allamuchy State Park,** which is located in a rugged area of the state. This vast park—more than 9,200 acres altogether—surprisingly straddles the busy lanes of Route 80. (Part of Allamuchy State Park is in Sussex County and can be accessed from the northern side.) But you will neither hear nor think of the highway when you are in the depths of these woodlands. There are 15 miles of trails through this wilderness, several of which lead to pristine bodies of water. Much of it is hardwood forest, but there are also swamplands and hemlocks, and it is a real climb to the top of the Allamuchy mountain.

The hike to **Deer Park Pond** is a dandy if your objective is being "away from it all." These remote forest trails are a natural area and have no facilities; take the map you'll find at the entrance and scan it carefully. The trek to the 46-acre pond is through a fern-filled woodland on a pleasant, unpaved—but not too difficult—trail. There is lots of wildlife, including wild turkeys and deer, and the work of beavers is evident when you come to the pond. (Look for their lodges in the pond.)

Just south of Allamuchy State Park is **Stephens State Park,** which lies on both sides of the Musconetcong River and the Morris Canal. Here you'll find one very pretty route for walking called the Highland Trail. You can also visit the Canal and Saxon Falls, two picturesque sites. Unlike Allamuchy, this park offers a variety of picnic and playground facilities and other amenities. Both parks have beautiful Warren County scenery. You can decide which one fits your needs and timeframe.

Information about both state parks is available at the office in Stephens State Park or from Mountain State Parks at 800 Willow Grove Street in Hackettstown. Telephone: 908-852-3790.

16·
CHESTER AREA

The Black River.

Exploring the Black River

⚜ HOW TO GET THERE

Hacklebarney State Park

From Route 80, take exit 27 (Route 206) south for about five miles to Chester, then west onto Route 513 (also called Route 24) for 1.2 miles. Turn left at the bridge after Cooper Mill onto Hacklebarney State Park Road and continue for another three miles. The park entrance is on the left.

Black River County Park:
Cooper Mill and Kay Environmental Center

For Cooper Mill, take Route 80 to Route 206 south to Chester; turn right onto Route 513 (Route 24) for 1.2 miles to Cooper Mill on the left. For the Kay Environmental Center, do the same as above, but continue on Route 206 south past Chester for about 1.5 miles. Turn right onto Pottersville Road and go nine-tenths of a mile to entrance.

Black River Wildlife Management Area (rail trail)

Take Route 80 to Route 206 south to Chester; turn left onto Route 513 (also called Main Street), then left (west) on Oakdale Road. Go 1.1 mile and turn right at the "Y" onto Pleasant Hill Road. You'll find the trail head is immediately after the driveway of Our Lady of Mt. Carmel Church.

The Black River virtually defines the green acres within the Chester region of Morris County. Not only is it a continuing presence in these areas, but it also gives its name to parklands and trails. Along its winding course (it finally flows into the Raritan River in Somerset County), it crosses the Black River Wildlife Management Area in the north, then moves swiftly across the Black River County Park (where it powers a grist mill) and through a dramatic gorge in Hacklebarney State Park.

It is difficult to imagine that this now peaceful river was once an industrial site. In fact, beginning in the late eighteenth century, iron mines were dug along its shores, mills were constructed, and a railroad to transport iron ore to the nearby Chester Furnace was built.

We thought it would be interesting and fun to explore the river—from its shores—as it widens and narrows at its various points of public access. The best access spots are two parks that offer unusually scenic walking trails. The third, the Black River Wildlife Management Area, has few marked paths (with the exception of a rail trail) and is best suited to experienced walkers with a topographic map in hand. We recommend it as an "extra" for those who have time and enjoy a challenge.

Within **Hacklebarney State Park** the Black River meanders and cascades, creating a spectacular gorge. Deep hemlocks and giant boulders line the banks of the river—which moves surprisingly fast here—and the terrain is quite rugged and steep. The park totals 890 acres, including some six miles of footpaths winding along the river and through the woods (a large section of the park is reserved for hunting).

Why the curious name of "Hacklebarney"? A colorful claim is that a local iron ore foreman named Barney Tracey was often heckled for his ill humor; "Heckle Barney" eventually evolved into "Hacklebarney." Another theory is that the name has a Native American derivation, meaning "to put wood on the ground" (i.e., to start a fire). An interesting footnote concerning the history of Hacklebarney: the parkland was in part donated by the Borie family, one of whose members (Susan Peterson Borie) survived the *Titanic* disaster.

We recommend a lovely three-mile hillside / river trail through a white pine, spruce, and hemlock forest with huge rocks. Though the trail is unmarked (its official name is the Black River Trail), it is easy to locate; you turn left past the parking area and walk down grand flights of stone steps. The path climbs up and down and you cross the river over rustic wooden bridges. Along the rocky banks you might see occasional anglers, particularly in an area called Three Pools; indeed, the river is stocked annually and trout fishing is popular. One particularly scenic spot is a waterfall, where you can sit on a rock and enjoy the view. The trail eventually ascends away from the river up a steep hill and back to the parking lot.

Needless to say, this is a wonderful spot for anyone open to adventure, including children. Some find the tall and uneven boulders irresistible for climbing, though slippery at times. In addition to walking and fishing (swimming is not allowed, though we did see people wading in shallow pools), there are waterside picnic tables (nicely spaced to afford some privacy), a children's playground, and a platform for wildlife viewing. The most spectacular time to visit is fall, though the park is beautiful at all times. (Summers can be buggy.)

Hacklebarney is open year-round daily, dawn to dusk, though the Visitor Center (where you can pick up maps and information on wildlife) is closed in winter. Fees on weekends only, from Memorial Day to Labor Day. Telephone: 908-879-5677.

🐝 **Black River County Park** is right near Hacklebarney—in fact, almost attached to it. Within its 510 acres is a great diversity of vegetation, from a hemlock ravine to hardwood forests filled with rhododendrons and beautiful meadows dotted with wildflowers. It is home to many birds and butterflies, as well as foxes, rabbits, squirrels, even coyotes and occasional bears.

You can enter the park at both **Cooper Mill** and the **Kay Environmental Center.** The picturesque Cooper Mill (1826), the oldest grist mill in Morris County and recently restored as a museum, offers stone-grinding demonstrations. The Kay Environmental Center, which provides public nature conservancy programs, is located on property once owned by the Kay family. (Elizabeth Kay was a great nature enthusiast and benefactor.) A number of inviting walking trails, described in the trail guide, can be reached from either site, including a 3.6-mile out-and-back river gorge trail that connects the two.

We chose to embark on this blue-blaze trail at Cooper Mill. Here the river is particularly vigorous, dropping dramatically into the gorge. You follow a small path toward the rushing water, climb up a raised embankment (a remnant of the railroad era), and proceed along a narrow-gauge rail bed for the first mile or so. You'll find yourself in a woodland of tall oaks and tulip trees, flowering shrubs, and wildflowers. The river swirls around large black boulders, making a roaring sound, and widens into a little pond with waterlilies and ducks.

When you've gone a bit over a mile you come to a junction where a sign points to the Kay Environmental Center (eight-tenths of a mile ahead). Here you have a choice. For a shorter and less arduous option, continue on the blue-blazed path to the Center; if you wish to explore the magnificent Black River Gorge hemlock ravine and don't mind walking an additional 1.5 miles in fairly rugged terrain, follow the unmarked wooded road to the right. (Directions are found in the guide.) Either way, you'll eventually come to open meadows surrounding the Center. Their flowering dogwoods, shrubs, and wildflowers attract a variety of migrating birds and butterflies—quite a vision, especially in spring. A circular trail winds around the grass, enabling you to experience this lovely spot more fully.

The trails in the Black River Park are open daily, dawn to dusk, year-round. Cooper Mill is open weekends May to October, and Friday to Tuesday in July and August. The Kay Environmental Center is open daily, all year. Telephone: Cooper Mill, 908-879-5463; Kay Environmental Center, 908-879-0566.

🌛 The **Black River Wildlife Management Area** encompasses 3,000 acres or so of woods and freshwater marshes and fields left in their natural state. Here the Black River is not the fast-moving power force it becomes as it heads southwest into the Black River Park and Hacklebarney; rather, it appears to be a slow, quiet stream. Its surrounding terrain is mostly unmarked—except for a rail trail—and walkers or birders (waterfowl and other migratory species are plentiful) have to make their own way.

The one walking trail we recommend is on a four-mile section of the abandoned Chester Branch of the railroad. This easy, mostly flat, unpaved, and quite picturesque woodland walk parallels the river, which is visible through the trees. The path ends at Ironia Road in Chester, where you can either make arrangements to be met by car or return on foot back to your starting point. Of course, you can also decide to take just a portion of the walk.

Note that during fall, hunters occasionally pass through on their way to more remote sections of the park; if that makes you nervous, you might prefer coming at other times of the year.

If you want to be more adventurous, you can explore the Black River Wildlife Management Area from other access points. One we found especially scenic is also off Pleasant Hill Road, about one mile after the Pleasant Hill Cemetery. You'll see a sign for Green Acres Wildlife Management Area on your right. Beyond is a large parking area leading to unusually beautiful cornfields and natural woodlands.

These parklands are always open, year-round, dawn to dusk. For more information (and to procure a topographic map, should you wish one) contact the New Jersey Division of Fish, Game, and Wildlife at 609-292-2965.

17·
CLINTON AREA

View of Round Valley State Park.

*Green Hunterdon: Walking
through a Tranquil River Gorge,
a Fitness Forest Trail, a Naturalistic
Arboretum, and a Lakeside Park*

 HOW TO GET THERE

Ken Lockwood Gorge Wildlife Management Area

From I-78, take exit 17 onto Route 31 north to Route 513 north, past the village of High Bridge. About 2 miles beyond the entrance to Voorhees State Park (see below) turn right onto Hoffman's Crossing Road, cross the little bridge, take an immediate right (River Road), and continue straight to the gorge.

Voorhees State Park

Same directions as above. The entrance to Voorhees State Park is on your left, a couple of miles after High Bridge.

Hunterdon County Arboretum

From I-78, take exit 16 onto Route 31 south, continuing for about four miles. Make a U turn at Stanton Station Road and go north on Route 31 for about one-fourth mile. The arboretum is on your right.

Round Valley State Park

From I-78, take exit 20A onto Route 22; continue onto Route 629 (which merges with Route 22), and follow signs to park entrance.

Hunterdon County offers some of New Jersey's most scenic vistas, with its rolling countryside of farmlands and villages, picturesque waterways, parks, and deep woods. Much of the region remains quite unspoiled, with few of the unsightly real estate developments found in far too many places, making it a particularly inviting destination for a day's exploration. The following walks are located in the environs of Clinton, a quaint, historic town with old houses and antique shops.

The **Ken Lockwood Gorge Wildlife Management Area** is serenely set in a deep wilderness along the south branch of the Raritan River, at the end of an unpaved road. All is quiet in this peaceful hemlock forest, except for the sounds of flowing water as it winds its way through the gorge, creating small waterfalls here and there. The clear, pristine river is surrounded by tall trees lining its steep embankments; giant boulders are strewn about, in the water and along the shoreline.

The 260-acre rustic site is maintained especially for fishing, and you might well encounter an occasional fisherman as you wend your way along the 2.5-mile path that parallels the river. (We are told there is an abundance of stocked trout, as well as bass and sunfish.) But walkers and birders also come, as do photographers now and again (we saw one trying to capture the exquisite beauty of light filtering through the trees). We recommend this idyllic walk at any time of the year, though you may find the access road to the gorge closed on certain wintry days. Spring and fall are ideal times, of course, when the vegetation is particularly sparkling; on summer days you'll find the shaded path a welcome respite from the heat.

Though this is an out-and-back trail, you can explore the other side of the river if you're feeling particularly adventuresome—not something we necessarily suggest, however. If you do, be sure to walk across with great caution, choosing carefully the best rocks to use as your bridge.

The gorge is open daily, year-round, from dawn to dusk. There are no concessions in this wilderness and no entrance fee. Telephone: 908-637-4125.

Nearby **Voorhees State Park** provides a different kind of nature experience, beautiful in its own way, though certainly less wild and rugged. Here, woodlands of tall, majestic trees alternate with well-tended open green areas, creating a feeling of spaciousness. The 640-acre park is quite hilly—it actually houses an observatory at its highest elevation (840 feet) from which visitors can explore the night sky and other astronomic phenomena. You can drive through the park to a number of scenic overlooks with magnificent views of the surrounding countryside.

Voorhees Park is situated on land which had been, until 1929, a farm property owned by a former state governor. Once it became a public park, trees were planted and roads, trails, shelters, and picnic/camp areas created. Today the park contains four walking/biking trails, as well as one exclusively for serious hiking; there is also a fitness circuit, one we especially recommend.

After you park your car at the entrance, pick up a map. It will tell you about each and every park offering. (Note that some areas are open to hunting and fishing in season.) For a change of pace (and to test how fit you really are!), you might try the fitness parcourse. With its 18 exercise stations spaced along a one-mile wooded path, this trail is a real workout for the total physical fitness buff. Each station comes with its specific instructions; a course marker, and apparatus where necessary. You'll find every type of activity, from stretching and warming up, to balancing, muscle strengthening, and cardiovascular conditioning, and you can monitor your heartbeat at regular intervals, following the directions provided. Of course, you can go at your own pace, pick and choose which exercises you wish to do, or simply walk (instead of run) from one station to the next. For obvious reasons, this trail is hardly ever crowded, making it appealingly peaceful as just a walk in the woods.

The park is open year-round daily, dawn to dusk. Telephone: 908-638-6969.

Our next walk takes you a few miles to the south, through the unusually pretty **Hunterdon County Arboretum.** Note that when we last visited, we found the road directions to this place somewhat confusing. The sign pointing to the arboretum from Route 31 south was misleading; it should have indicated a U turn and not what appeared to be a right-hand turn. But once there, we felt it was well worth the effort.

This 73-acre arboretum is on a site once occupied by one of New Jersey's largest nurseries. It includes formal gardens as well as fields, wetlands, and forests, where you can walk on mowed, grassy paths, enjoying a wide variety of plants and wildlife, too. The arboretum beyond the enclosed area has a more naturalistic ambience than most, with few marked trees and shrubs, with either English or, for that matter, Latin designations.

At the administration building next to the parking lot you can pick up a map of the grounds and a self-guiding nature trail. A formal display garden, recently fenced in to keep out the ever-increasing deer population, comes first. Here is quite a collection of ornamental grasses, katsura, crabapple and other flowering trees, and colorful annuals and perennials. A 100-year-old gazebo (brought here in 1978 from a nearby estate) is surrounded with yet more flower gardens, a butterfly garden, and a good assortment of herbs.

When you leave the fenced-in garden (be sure to close the gate carefully!), you enter a wetlands area, complete with willows, a pond (home to many frogs), skunk cabbage, cattails, and a nice boardwalk from which to view it all. The boardwalk leads to a network of walking trails, mostly flat and easy to negotiate. Along the way you'll see grapevines, cork trees, tall sycamores, and delicately beautiful dogwoods, among other varieties. Although in a few spots you can still see trees standing in rows (reminiscent of the past nursery era), most appear in random, informal arrangements. In some open areas are multiflora rose bushes; in fall and winter birds are often seen flying around them, attracted to the rose hips.

The arboretum is open daily, year-round, from 8 A.M. to dusk. (Note that the park office is closed on Sundays and holidays.) There is no entrance fee. Telephone: 908-782-1158.

Undoubtedly the most striking feature in nearby **Round Valley State Park** is its dazzling reservoir, all 4,000 acres of it. One of the largest and deepest lakes in the entire state, it was created to conserve water and opened to the public in the 1970s for recreational use. A dam separates the main reservoir (where there is both fishing and boating) from the swimming area and its long, broad sandy beach. Judging by the size of the adjacent parking lot, the beach is popular in the summer. The reservoir, surrounded on three sides by the hilly terrain of Cushetunk Mountain, also provides a picturesque setting for some inviting walking and hiking trails.

Round Valley Recreation Area, as it is officially known, is an unusually well kept park with vast expanses of grass and woodlands—in some places, quite rugged and steep. There are four marked trails—including a long (10-mile), fairly rocky trek for strong hikers, bikers, and horseback riders that crosses through both open and densely wooded areas. For a less arduous experience, try either the Pine Tree Trail or the Family Hiking and Biking Trail, both one-mile loops good for birdwatching in pretty woodlands. Of course, a nice alternative is to go on your own off-season walk along the lovely lakeside beach. You will have the place to yourself (as we did, on one sparkling September day) and be able to enjoy the spectacular water and mountain views in peace.

Be sure to pick up the park brochure (with complete descriptions of trails, picnic, camping, boating, fishing sites, and other offerings) at the park entrance.

Round Valley is open daily, year-round, dawn to dusk. Entrance fees only during the summer, from Memorial Day to Labor Day. Telephone: 908-236-6355.

18·
RINGOES
AND MILFORD
REGIONS

Unionville Vineyards, Ringoes.

*Vineyard Walks:
Western New Jersey's
Prettiest Wineries*

HOW TO GET THERE

Alba Vineyard

From I-78 west, take exit 7, Bloomsbury, to Route 173 west; go 1.3 miles to Route 639 west (bear left). Continue 2.8 miles to stop sign and go straight on Route 627. Winery is in Milford, 2.5 miles further on the right at number 269 Route 627.

Amwell Valley Vineyard

From I-78, take exit 17 and go south on Route 31. After it joins with Route 202, turn east on Route 514 (Old York Road) in Ringoes. Follow signs to vineyard at 80 Old York Road.

Unionville Vineyards

This vineyard is very near Amwell Valley Vineyard. From Old York Road return to Routes 202/31 and go south for one long block. Turn east on Wertsville Road in Ringoes. Take the second right (Rocktown Road), and the vineyard at number 9 Rocktown Rd. is the first driveway you'll come to.

Walking in vineyards is an unusual pleasure. While you may have enjoyed glorious vineyards in California or Europe, you needn't go so far afield. In the past ten years more than a dozen vineyards have begun operating in New Jersey. They offer the walker a different and delightful setting.

Most vineyards occupy hilly terrain, with bright sunshine and gentle breezes a requisite part of the setting. The paths through the neat rows of growing vines are heady with the fragrance of grapes in season. The best time to visit is late summer and early fall, though vineyards are inviting in spring and summer, too. You'll find that a number of amenities add to your pleasure: wine festivals, watching wine being made (no, we didn't see anyone stomping on the grapes with bare feet!), and the requisite tastings at the end of your walk. All of the vineyards sell their wine—and other wine related items—on the spot. The three vineyards described here were our favorites in this part of the state, both for their natural beauty and for the gracious reception we received from the owners. If you would like to visit the vineyards when there are special events going on, you can telephone the New Jersey Wine Line at 800-524-0043.

 Alba Vineyard is the farthest west of these three wineries and one of the oldest. Quite near the Delaware River, it occupies a very hilly and lovely spot in this pleasantly bucolic region of the state. From the top of the hill you can see expansive views of the Garden State below you. The lovely ambience of this site—which covers 90 acres—is created by the paths that wind among the staked vines up and down and around the hill. This is a working business, and part of its appeal is its seriousness; there are tractors and piles of fencing and other signs of the hard work that goes into running a vineyard—beauty and fragrance aside. You will enjoy seeing the ever-expanding rows of grapevines; they have recently added six additional acres of rocky hillside and hedgerows. (This is not a walk for hill haters; it is quite steep.) When you descend, you can taste their wine in the converted stone 190-year-old dairy barn or in a picnic area under an arbor, or in the wine cellar itself. Tours are available. The vineyard is open Wednesday, Thursday, Friday, and Sunday from noon to 5 P.M.; Saturdays 10 A.M. to 6 P.M. Telephone: 908-995-7800.

Amwell Valley Vineyard is in Ringoes, in a region not too far away from Alba Vineyards as the crow flies (but it is easiest to return to Route I-78 to get there). This is a gentler-sloping landscape with a very bucolic atmosphere. We enjoyed walking through the fields with intermittent areas of staked grapevines. The vistas and buzzing bees and warmth of sun and growing things was indeed inviting. For those walkers who would like a change from wooded paths to open fields, this is an ideal spot. Amwell Valley Vineyard is open Saturday and Sunday from 1 P.M. to 5 P.M. and on other days by appointment. Telephone: 908-788-5852.

Unionville Vineyards is nearby. It is a much-admired vineyard, having received a "Best Winery in New Jersey" award from the *New York Times* and various other kudos—over 250 of them. Our guess is that it is not just the wine that they are admiring. The atmosphere is unusually pleasing. Though the vineyard itself is less than ten years old, its marvelous old dairy barn—where you can watch the process of making wine from a glassed-in second level—dates back, in part, to 1858. The owners have made the entire vineyard inviting to visitors. You can walk through the beautiful setting of rolling hills and fields and staked grapevines at your leisure and find yourself wonderfully lost in the maze of red grapes and white grapes and hybrids. The Amwell Valley is a gentle landscape, and we are happy to hear that more and more of it is being saved for farm and vineyard land by conservationists.

The vineyard is open Thursday to Sunday from 11 A.M. to 4 P.M. for tastings and tours; you can visit at any time and wander around on your own. There are numerous special events. Telephone: 908-788-0400.

There are a number of other vineyards in the vicinity. You can pick up a flyer at any of the wineries described above and find out about additional sites and events.

19·
SOMERSET
COUNTY

*Winter
Getaway:
Indoor
and Outdoor
Pleasures*

Sourland Mountain Preserve.

❧ HOW TO GET THERE

Doris Duke Gardens

From Route 80, take I-287 south to exit 17. Take Route 206 south; when you reach the Somerville Circle (junction of Routes 206 and 202) continue on Route 206 for another 1.75 miles. The entrance to the gardens is on your right.

Sourland Mountain Preserve

From Route 80, take I-287 south to exit 17, onto Route 206 south. At Somerville Circle continue on Route 206 south for 8.5 miles, turning right onto Route 601 south. Drive a little over one mile and turn right on East Mountain Road. The preserve entrance is about one mile down the road, on the left-hand side.

A wonderful time to visit gardens is winter—indoor gardens, that is. For, while the outside world is cold and somewhat colorless, greenhouse oases—with their brilliant blossoms and warm temperatures (to accommodate tropical plants)—offer a cheery, springlike contrast.

Winter is also an ideal time to walk in the woods. In the quiet stillness of the season you can admire the stark beauty of unadorned trees and feel invigorated by the cold air while protected from its most chilling winds. (Another winter pleasure, a nice cup of hot tea in a cozy place, might follow your brisk winter walk.)

Below are two such sites within Somerset County's pretty countryside: a magnificent indoor garden considered to be among New Jersey's treasures, and a wonderfully natural woodland. While both can be visited and enjoyed at most times of the year, consider them as especially nice winter outings, either as a complementary pair or as individual excursions.

❧ The **Doris Duke Gardens** in Somerville—a major tourist attraction for which well-in-advance reservations are a must—are a spectacular group of interconnected conservatories. Situated on what was once the estate of the tobacco heiress, these 2,700 acres are accessible through imposing iron gates topped with black eagles. Inside are lush grounds of lawns, lakes, wooded parklands, exotic flowers, and roaming deer. You are met at the entrance by a van and taken directly to the gardens for a guided tour.

The ornate glass conservatories were built in the late nineteenth century in an Edwardian style. Inside are eleven separate gardens, each with a different theme representing traditions of various countries and cultures.

The original gardens were restored in the late 1950s and opened to the public in 1964. You walk from one room to the next (with the guide and other visitors), covering about a mile in roughly an hour's time.

The first stop, the Italian garden, is a wonderful beginning. Luxuriant blossoms of mimosa, orange and pink bougainvillea, bird-of-paradise, Italian statuary and fountains, and gravel paths give it an aura of nineteenth-century romance.

Next comes the American Colonial garden, more orderly and classical, with well-groomed hedges, hanging white and pink petunias, and dazzling camellias, azaleas, and magnolias. White latticework and neat, brick-trimmed paths add to the colonial flavor.

The next conservatory—the Edwardian garden—is filled with brilliant orchids of every kind, supplied by other greenhouses on the grounds. White, magenta, and purple blossoms are set off by the deep green of rubber plants and palms in the warm, humid surroundings. This is the quintessential garden of late nineteenth century romantic novels.

From there you enter the formal French garden. Eighteenth-century-style latticework surrounds this charming formal arrangement of stone paths, ivy-festooned columns, delicate fountains, and tiny niches. A special feature is a very large fleur-de-lis made from colorful flowers, the kind of decorative element you find in the elaborate gardens of French chateaus.

Then comes a group of intimate, colorful English gardens, including a rockery, a topiary garden, an herbal knot garden, and a pretty flower garden.

In startling contrast is the almost monochromatic desert garden with dusty, dirt floor and giant cacti reaching up to the glass ceiling. The aura is that of the American Southwest: brown and gray-green tones in knobby, fantastic shapes, giving the visitor the sense of wild, untamed nature.

The Chinese garden, a favorite among visitors, is a peaceful oasis for quiet reflection. Here you can see wonderful rock formations, mysterious grottos for contemplation, and delicate arching stone bridges surrounded by leaning willows and bamboos. A small pond is filled with golden carp.

The Japanese garden is a stylized, traditional arrangement including an elegant teahouse, tiny streams, a miniature wood bridge, and gnarled trees in fascinating shapes. A small contemplation area features carefully raked sand in swirling, wavelike patterns.

You then come to the striking Indo-Persian garden representing an Islamic palace garden. Here, in a setting evoking tales from exotic lands, is a romantic reflecting pool surrounded by beautiful flowers in geometric patterns. The air is filled with the aroma of orange blossoms. You will want to linger in this lush ambience!

The tropical rain forest garden contains jungle plants of all shades of green, including banana plants, huge elephant ears, and Spanish moss. Look for the occasional orchid hidden in the dense foliage.

You finally come to the semitropical garden. Many kinds of purple flowers decorate the edges of the brick paths and terrace, surrounded by gloxinias and gardenias in large urns and hanging bougainvillea. Tree ferns from volcanic regions of Hawaii and New Zealand and the one-of-a-kind bird-of-paradise plants add a touch of the exotic.

The Doris Duke Gardens are open October 1 through May 31, daily, noon to 4 P.M. (closed on major holidays). Reservations are necessary. Entrance fee. Telephone: 908-722-3700.

From the genteel, contained environment of the Duke Gardens we now go to the wilderness of **Sourland Mountain Preserve,** 2,000 acres of pristine forests and rough, rocky terrain. The preserve is located within Sourland Mountain, a 10-mile-long and 4-mile-wide undeveloped ridge, apparently so-named by early German settlers for its acidic and rocky land. (Its unusual name might also be derived from "sorrel-land," as these pioneers described its reddish-brown soil.) Parts of the ridge are high enough (at almost 600 feet) to permit views of Manhattan's skyline.

The preserve itself, a fairly recent addition to the Somerset County park system, offers a liberating experience. Here you are free to hike and explore at will, encountering only a few people here and there (and just an occasional mountain bike, horse, or dog). Sections of the preserve are quite remote, in fact not accessible from the marked trails. There are difficult-to-reach boulder fields, consisting of giant igneous rock formations that are fascinating to explore. Naturalists are sometimes available on Saturdays to lead walks to such sites.

But you need not go to these lengths to experience the preserve. The three marked trails that wind through a deep forest of beech, tulip, and oak trees offer wonderful walking and hiking. They interconnect at various junctions, too, so that you can sample bits and pieces or entire sections, as you choose. (Before starting out, be sure to pick up a trail map near the parking area.)

The easiest and shortest path is the Pondside Trail (marked with a circle), a half-mile loop over gentle slopes; or follow the triangle markings for the Maple Flat Trail, just over a mile of scenic woodland. The most challenging, the Ridge Trail (rectangle), covers 3.3 miles over somewhat steep woodsy terrain, with streams and boardwalks and fields of tall reeds along the way. This trail affords panoramic vistas, too, making it well worth the effort.

Sourland Mountain Preserve is open daily, year-round, from dawn to dusk. There is no entrance fee. Telephone: 908-722-1200.

20·
DELAWARE AND
RARITAN CANAL
REGION

Biking along the Delaware and Raritan Canal.

Along a Peaceful Canal
and through a Rose Garden

🌿 HOW TO GET THERE

Delaware & Raritan Canal State Park, Main Canal

From Route 287, take exit 12 to Canal Road (south of Bound Brook).

Kingston Branch Loop Trail

This trail is located at the south end of the above canal, just north of Lake Carnegie in Princeton, at the intersection of Route 27. Park at the John Fleemer Preserve.

Colonial Park

From Route 287, take exit 12 at Weston Canal Road, go south on Canal Road; turn left before the bridge and continue along the canal. Turn left onto Weston Road, right onto Mettlers Road. Follow signs for the park.

The walks described below are set in rural parts of the Somerset country-side. Featuring walks along a picturesque canal reminiscent of another era and a stroll through a charming rose garden, they will appeal especially to those with a romantic bent.

🌿 You can begin your wonderful walk along the **Main Canal of the Delaware & Raritan Canal** at South Bound Brook and Weston Canal Road and walk (or bike) south for some 30 miles, should you so desire. For a shorter version, cross the canal over a number of small bridges at various intervals along the way, enabling you to make a loop.

Work on the D&R Canal was begun in 1830 to transport freight between New York and Philadelphia long before the railroad boom. For four years a largely Irish immigrant workforce dug manually the 44-mile-long Main Canal and its 22-mile feeder, a huge feat considering the canal's 50 to 75 foot width and its 6 to 7 foot depth. Until the end of the nineteenth century, this navigational canal was one of the country's busiest, especially during the 1860s and '70s when it was mostly used for transporting Pennsylvania coal to fuel New York's surging industrial economy. The canal's heyday was more or less over by the turn of the century, when the railroad became the preferred mode of transport, and it was finally closed in 1932. For a time it served as a water supply system and, happily for us, was eventually turned into a recreational state park, with some of the most enchanting trails anywhere in the state.

Our spectacular walk is along the raised towpath, once trod by the mules that hauled the barges between New York, Trenton, and Philadelphia. It is a narrow, flat, tree-lined oasis where you're only aware of reflections, birdsong, and delicious air. Although one of the state's most popular venues for canoeing, jogging, hiking, and birding (some 160 species have been identified), we saw virtually no one on any of our walks there. If you have an interest in history, you will be fascinated by the many little nineteenth-century bridges and bridge-tender houses, hand-built stone culverts, and remnants of the original 14 locks you will see along the way. We particularly recommend this outing in spring and fall, when the views are glorious and there are no insects flying about.

The Kingston Branch Loop Trail is a highly scenic 3.7-mile loop that follows the route of a narrow rail corridor one way, crosses the canal over a small wooden bridge, then circles back on the canal towpath. (Most other railroad beds that have been converted into walking paths are linear, rather than circular, making this one quite special.)

Among the sites you'll encounter are a bog and a surprisingly large quarry situated on a hillside where, incidentally, George Washington actually wrote his famous speech "The Farewell to the Troops." The quarry, begun in the 1860s and still functioning today, was one of the main reasons that the railroad came here in the first place. It yielded the trap rock used to pave many city streets in New Jersey and New York, some of which you may well have walked on. The path is flat, with a fine stone dust surface that is very pleasant underfoot.

For general information on the D&R Canal State Park, call 732-873-3050.

We now take you just down the road to **Colonial Park** and its beautiful rose garden. Actually, there are three distinct gardens within these 476-acre grounds—a fragrance and sensory garden, a perennial garden, and the rose garden, which we especially recommend. All are part of a more extensive arboretum with clearly marked flowering trees and shrubs and evergreens.

The tiny Fragrance and Sensory Garden demonstrates how plants can appeal to all the senses. Included are aromatic, prickly, or spongy varieties that can be experienced through smell and touch, or even taste (though we don't recommend trying the latter). Here Braille plaques identify an eclectic selection, including lavender, mint, and fuzzy lamb's ear, as well as more exotic plants. The ambience is intimate and quiet, with flat walkways and cool, shaded benches inviting you to rest for a moment.

The four-acre Perennial Garden surrounds a dainty gazebo (a delightful setting for a picnic, if it is not being used for bridal parties). The colorful array of ornamental grasses, trees, shrubs, and perennials is clearly identified and arranged for year-round enjoyment.

The magnificent Rudolf W. van der Goot Rose Garden more than lives up to its impressive title. One of 24 nationwide test gardens recognized by All-America Rose Selections, it was created in 1971 by the man whose name it bears, the first horticulturalist of the Park Commission. And what a rose garden it is! This one-acre enclosed wonder, considered one of the ten best gardens of its kind in the country, is a virtual encyclopedia of roses.

The collection, arranged in three sections complete with reflecting pool, clipped hedges, and brick-edged paths, includes 4,000 rosebushes (275 varieties) in bloom from early June well into the fall. The aptly named Grandmother's Garden contains lush displays of old hybrid perpetual and tea roses, some dating as far back as the 1820s; the compact Dutch Garden, in the style of a formal rose garden in Holland, is designed to allow close inspection of the roses and dwarf candytuft outlining the beds; and the Center Garden features beds of floribunda and grandiflora roses radiating from a central walkway. Any rose fancier will find this a blissful stroll, with a touch of romance from a different time and place.

The gardens in Colonial Park are open daily, from 8 A.M. to sunset. There is no entrance fee, though a small donation is appreciated. Telephone: 732-873-2459.

21·
ROUTE 1,
MIDDLESEX
COUNTY AREA

Bamboo Forest at Rutgers Display Gardens.

Well-Kept Secrets: Nature Walks in a Bamboo Forest, a University Woodland, and a Lakeside Bird Sanctuary

 **HOW TO GET THERE**

Rutgers Display Gardens and Frank G. Helyar Woods

Both sites are part of Rutgers University's Cook College Campus located near Route 1. From the New Jersey Turnpike, take exit 9 to Route 1 south toward New Brunswick. Exit at Ryder's Lane, cross under the highway to the opposite side and follow signs.

Plainsboro Preserve of the New Jersey Audubon Society

From Route 1 as above, exit at Scudders Mill Road and go to the fifth traffic light (Dey Road). Turn left onto Dey Road and head east for about 1.5 miles to Scotts Corner Road. Turn left and go for about one-fourth mile, past Community Park on the left. Entrance to the preserve is on your left.

Route 1 in Middlesex County, a busy corridor to Princeton from the turnpike, has, surprisingly, several special spots for walking very near to it. You will not hear traffic nor feel the urban vibes of highway in these oases, for which we can fervently thank Rutgers University, the town and county, and the Audubon Society. Each walk is unusual, not just for its proximity to urban civilization, but for its own special ambience.

For example, a walk through a bamboo forest is unlike any other woodland walk. Part of **Rutgers Display Gardens**, the university's teaching and research gardens, this forest walk is an original experience. If you have ever seen ancient Asian art with its fearsome tigers creeping through bamboo forests, you will recognize this mysterious setting. There are hundreds of bamboo trees here. They grow very straight and thin, and very close to one another, making geometric patterns against the sky, their tall straight trunks a lovely shade of—yes, bamboo color. They leave a creamy, pale carpet of leaves below, and walking on them feels soft and delightful. A professor at the university planted them many years ago (only a few of them because he needed some bamboo poles), but then nature took its course and the result is amazing.

While you are at this site you might also visit other sections of the Display Gardens. These include some 25 or 30 acres of interesting environments: research gardens, specimen gardens, woods, both aquatic and thematic gardens—each different from the next. There are Asian tree collections, a pink dogwood collection (visit in spring), the largest holly collection in the nation, and other tree groups, in addition to our favorite bamboo forest. The atmosphere is open and pleasant and you will feel free to walk around wherever you like.

Rutgers University sites are open daily from 8:30 A.M. to dusk, May through September, and from 8:30 A.M. to 4:30 P.M. October through April. Telephone: 732-932-8451.

The **Frank G. Helyar Woods** is also a part of Rutgers University. This is a lovely mixed hardwood forest that, despite its proximity to the highway, is a virgin woodland. Today it is used only for teaching and research, and as an inviting site for walking. The woods cover 41 acres; there is a nice walking trail—a loop of a little over a mile round-trip. (You can pick up a guide to the trees; they are numbered but not otherwise identified.)

Leave your car at the log building and enter these dark and inviting woods. Almost 50 different types of trees grow here, ranging from black or swamp white oak (some are 90 feet tall), to hickory, "Tree of Heaven," and chestnuts. In fact, there is a "chestnut graveyard" here, where once dozens of the great trees flourished. This is a birder's woods. You'll also come upon a wetland region featuring all sorts of swamp growth: ferns and greenbriar, spicebush and wild elderberry, and lots of indigenous trees. Climbing up a slight incline you'll even come to an "Indian Cave," which is really an old mine shaft left by prospectors looking for copper in the shale. Your lookout from the trail may include Weston's Mill Pond, now a reservoir but once a dammed waterway that provided power to a mill in the nineteenth century.

Plainsboro Preserve is a little farther along Route 1 toward Princeton. This site is certainly one of our favorites. These 631 acres in the heart of constantly encroaching sprawl are a delight. Though easily accessible, this preserve is just that: a preservation of nature where it is fast disappearing. This land of wonderfully varied habitats was saved and opened to the public only recently. There are more than five miles of trails, including a scenic shoreline walk along the banks of 50-acre McKormak Lake, a floodplain, wet meadows, a fine forest, wildflowers galore, butterflies, and birds, birds, birds. Some 150 species have been sighted here. (You'll find a self-guiding map and lists of nature's creatures at the new Environmental Education Center.) The pathways are soft, peach-colored, and sand-packed, bordered with such rarities as wild orchids or familiar bayberry. It is hard to conceive of such a quiet, tranquil environment in the midst of everything, but take our word for it and try this very special place for a walk.

Plainsboro Preserve is open from sunrise to sunset daily. Telephone: 609-897-9400.

22·
PRINCETON

Prospect Garden, Princeton University.

Princeton Pleasures: Campus Sculpture Walk, University Gardens, a Park-cum Arboretum, and a Historic Cemetery

⚜ HOW TO GET THERE

Princeton University

Take the New Jersey Turnpike to exit 9; take Route 1 south, then Route 571 west to Princeton. The main entrance is off Nassau Street, in the heart of Princeton.

Prospect Gardens

Located off Washington Road, on the Princeton University campus.

Marquand Park

Located off Lovers Lane. From Nassau Street, go south to Stockton Street (Route 206 south) and turn left on Lovers Lane. The park will be on your left.

Princeton Cemetery

Entrance is at the end of Greenview Avenue, off Wiggins Street (Wiggins runs parallel to Nassau Street).

⚘ There are many reasons to visit the town of Princeton. Of course, most people come to see the university and its famous campus, unquestionably one of the most beautiful in the country. But this picturesque town offers other pleasures as well, from leafy parks and lovely gardens to little-known historic sites. Following are some of the most inviting places—including a highly recommended campus walk—that make Princeton a wonderful day's outing.

Among our favorite walks are those that combine outdoor art with lovely natural surroundings. The **Princeton University** campus is a particularly pleasant place for walking and enjoying outdoor sculpture. Its shaded walkways, lawns, and Gothic buildings provide a unique setting for exhibiting art—and what a collection you'll find here! On display are more than twenty works by some of the twentieth century's most illustrious artists. The list reads like a "Who's Who," with such names as Picasso, Alexander Calder, George Rickey, David Smith, Henry Moore, Louise Nevelson, and Isamu Noguchi.

Before embarking on your self-guided tour, you'll want to pick up a campus map at the information desk near the entrance gate on Nassau Street, opposite Palmer Square. (Because cars are not allowed on campus, you should park at a meter in the street or at a parking lot.) The map plots out a walking tour indicating the main sites in numerical order. If you prefer, take a guided tour, given several times a day.

As you stroll about, enjoying the sculpture and natural surroundings (as well as the always fascinating scenes of college life around you), you'll see that each work has been carefully placed, in harmony with its setting. A bronze Henry Moore—"Oval with Points"—sits gracefully on the green (students can often be seen draped on its now burnished forms); George Rickey's gently undulating "Two Planes, Vertical Horizon II" catches the breezes on an open stretch of lawn; the jagged forms of Jacques Lipchitz's "Song of the Vowels," a soaring bronze suggesting a harpist, is framed by the university chapel and library; and Louise Nevelson's "Atmosphere and Environment X," a very tall Cor-Ten steel work of interlocking black, white, and gold geometric shapes, reflects surrounding shadows on sunny days.

The walk takes you through a large part of the campus, including the School of Architecture (to view Eduardo Paolozzi's imaginative "junk" sculpture, "Marok, Marok, Miosa"), the Engineering Quad, and even as far as some newer dormitory buildings near the train station. There you'll see one of the campus's favorite pieces, David Smith's "Cubi XIII," a nine-foot-high stainless steel work. If possible, you should also stop to see some indoor works—the famous head of Albert Einstein by the American/British sculptor Jacob Epstein (appropriately situated inside the physics library), or the African sculptures and European and American paintings in the fine art museum. (Look for the immediately recognizable Picasso in front of the building.)

The university campus is open year-round. Guided tours are offered daily and are free of charge; for information call 609-258-3603. Or you can pick up a map and walk around on your own.

✼ Besides its sculptures, the Princeton campus is also well endowed in terms of its greenery. One particularly delightful spot is **Prospect Gardens**, aptly named for its views to the east. The property includes a nineteenth-century Italianate mansion (occupied by university presidents from the late 1870s until 1968) and English-style gardens.

The garden is circular in design, with beds of brilliantly colored perennials and annuals surrounding a gracious fountain. Beyond the formal plantings are carefully tended lawns and magnificent specimen trees, some that have grown to more than 100 feet.

The flower garden (surrounded by an iron fence) is arranged in two tiers featuring many varieties, including a charming rose collection. Throughout the growing season you can enjoy a continuing array of bright blossoms—from daffodils, tulips, irises, peonies, and hyacinths that magically appear in spring, to summer daylilies and perennials, and early autumn chrysanthemums. It is easy to see why this romantic spot is a favorite site for wedding parties. The garden is also used for more traditional university functions.

Prospect Gardens, once part of a vast estate, is quite an intimate site, including just two acres; you'll find a visit here is more conducive to a leisurely stroll than an invigorating walk. You can savor this spot at all times of the year, especially in June, when the roses are in full bloom. Open daily, year-round, from dawn to dusk and free of charge. Telephone: 609-258-3455.

🌺 **Marquand Park** is one of those well-kept secrets. Who could imagine that just minutes from Princeton's bustling downtown you could find so idyllic a setting, one more reminiscent of a Constable painting than a town park? With its broad lawns and vistas, magnificent specimen trees and shrubs, and wooded glens, this 17-acre arboretum-cum park has very much the feel of a romantic English landscape.

In fact, the park has its roots in the nineteenth century, at a time when there was great interest in collecting unusual and exotic plants. From the mid-1800s, when this once farm property became a private estate, until it was donated to the town for public use (in 1953), its occupants were all horticulture enthusiasts. The original owner, a judge and Princeton professor of jursiprudence named Richard Field, spent years designing the grounds himself and engaged an English gardener to procure and plant trees and shrubs (some from remote locales); subsequent owners added yet more to an already rich collection.

Today you can stroll along a gravel path that winds about the grounds, or walk on soft grassy expanses, admiring some 200 species of domestic and foreign trees—Norway spruces, Japanese maples, evergreens from Crete and Syria, European larches, etc. (Everything is carefully labeled, so you need not be an expert botanist to identify the trees.) Some are among the largest and oldest in the state, such as the enormous cedar of Lebanon that was only 10 feet high when Field planted it in 1842, located on the edge of the property near the still privately owned manor house, and the giant empress tree, right at the park entrance. The wooded area also contains some imposing oaks, maples, hickories, and tulips—as well as flowering shrubs and carpets of wildflowers, a delight in spring.

This abundance of vegetation attracts birds, too, and you can look for cardinals, chickadees, woodpeckers, and migrating birds in season.

The park is open daily, year-round, from dawn to dusk. There is no entrance fee. Parking available. Telephone: 609-921-9480.

Being the historic town that it is, Princeton offers quite a number of interesting sites for visitors. Among our favorites is the **Princeton Cemetery**, a shady and serene corner property with some 17 acres to explore.

Because so many prominent historical figures are buried on these leafy grounds, the cemetery has, on occasion, been called the "Westminster Abbey of the United States." The list is quite fascinating, combining public—as well as less known—figures, from university presidents to politicians and signers of the Declaration of Independence; from writers and musicians to scholars and mathematicians. Even a U.S. president is buried here: Grover Cleveland, who lived in Princeton from 1897 to 1908. Though names like Stockton, Bayard, Terhune, and Leonard may not mean much to most visitors, these notable families are well represented here as part of the town's rich historical legacy.

Just beyond the entrance to the graveyard, you'll find a cemetery map with all the information you'll need, including history, notable gravemarkers, and who is buried where. The oldest section, along Wiggins and Witherspoon streets, is where you'll find the Presidents' Plot, the most visited of all the markers. Here, under lovely old trees, are the monuments of eleven former university presidents, including Aaron Burr Sr. (his is the oldest in the cemetery); his son Aaron Burr Jr., the vice president of the U.S. who engaged Alexander Hamilton in that infamous duel; and Jonathan Edwards, a noted clergyman. Others to look for include the writer John O'Hara, Sylvia Beach (original publisher of James Joyce's *Ulysses*), George H. Gallup (creator of the Gallup Poll), and Margaret Leonard (the first European child born in Princeton), and many more. You'll also come across some interesting epitaphs, as well. Among the wittiest: "I told you I was sick."

The Princeton Cemetery is open daily, year-round. Telephone: 609-924-1369.

 ## IN THE VICINITY
Princeton Battlefield State Park

For another taste of local history, stop at this park near the center of town, situated on the site of a Revolutionary War battle. Here, on January 3, 1777, George Washington's troops defeated a force of British Regulars.

Today it is a broad expanse of grass, where you can meander at will (there are no set paths), imagining the events that occurred 250 years ago. An inviting allée of evergreens greets you at the entrance. The park itself has few trees (and those are mostly on the edge) but nice country views. On the premises you can also visit historic Clark House, built in 1772, and now a museum.

The park is at 500 Mercer Street and is open from dawn to dusk daily, year-round. There is no entrance fee. Clark House is open Wednesday to Saturday, 10 A.M. to noon and 1 P.M. to 4 P.M.; Sunday, 1 P.M. to 4 P.M. Telephone: 609-921-0074.

23·
MERCER
COUNTY

*Along the
Delaware:
A Historic
Park,
a Canal
Walk, a
Corn Maze,
and a
Medicinal
Trail*

Washington Crossing State Park.

❧ HOW TO GET THERE

Washington Crossing State Park

From I-295, take exit 1 north (north of Trenton) to Route 29 north; take a right onto Route 546; the main entrance to the park is on your right, about half a mile away.

D&R Canal State Park *(Canal Walk along the Delaware)*

From the Visitor Center at Washington Crossing State Park, walk to Continental Lane (a grassy path in front of the center), go left, toward the river. At the end of Continental Lane, bear left a few feet, then right onto a paved path going south. This path leads to a pedestrian walking bridge over Route 29 and to the canal towpath. You can go left or right on the towpath.

Little Acres Corn Maze

The maze is located at Belle Mountain in Hopewell Township (Mercer County). Take Route 546 to Pennington and go one mile east. The maze is located off 546, between Twin Pines Airport and Manors Shopping Center.

In this historic region you can enjoy long stretches of the glorious Delaware River, with its surrounding farmlands and gentle hills. It was here that George Washington crossed the Delaware on Christmas night 1776, one of the great, dramatic moments in the Revolutionary War. Today a large and beautiful park, situated on both sides of the river, commemorates the event. Because of the nature of our book, we are mainly concerned with the Washington Crossing Park on the New Jersey side; however, we strongly recommend you also cross the river, drive a few miles north, and visit the wildlife preserve called Bowman's Hill (in the Pennsylvania section of the park) for a delightful trail walk and plants long used for medicinal purposes.

Back in the New Jersey farmlands just a few miles east of the Delaware, you'll also find an intriguing corn maze, which will amuse children and adults alike. Walking through a labyrinth of overgrown corn on a fine autumn day can be a real adventure!

❧ **Washington Crossing State Park,** the site where the Continental Army under General George Washington landed after that famous crossing in 1776, is a grand, 1,399-acre scenic park with rolling hills and magnificent river views. Offering everything from historic walking tours and a museum and interpretive center, to a delightful arboretum, nature trails, picknicking, camping, fishing, bicycling, and even horseback riding, it is the perfect spot for a day's outing—whether you're interested in seeing the banks the Continental Army climbed and the houses where they rested, or simply enjoying the beautiful natural environment.

Washington chose this particular crossing point for strategic reasons, for here his troops could pass, undetected. The battles they fought after this epic landing are considered the turning point of the war.

The park was established in 1912 and originally contained only 100 acres. Most of the amenities—the buildings, roads, trails, and picnic groves—were built in the 1930s, during the Works Project Administration (WPA) era.

Before setting forth on your park exploration, stop at the Visitor Center to pick up maps, brochures, listings of wildlife, and, if you like, information on tours. This building also houses the historic museum with its comprehensive exhibits of historical artifacts. Among the recommended stopping points are the Johnson Ferry House (which Washington and his staff occupied after the crossing); the Nelson House, located on the actual ferry site along the riverbank; and the George Washington Memorial Arboretum (adjacent to the Ferry House). This exquisite garden is popular in spring, when the dogwoods, crab apples, and ornamental cherries are at their peak; but with a wonderful collection of trees (all carefully labeled) indigenous to New Jersey, it is a rare treat at any time of year. (The park is particularly noted for its fall foliage.) Be sure to leave time to explore at least some of the park's 13 miles of trails.

The park is open daily during daylight hours throughout the year. There is no admission charge during the week. The Visitor Center, Nature Center, and historic houses are open Wednesday to Sunday, 9 A.M. to 4 P.M. Telephone: 609-737-0623.

For an inspiring waterside walk, we recommend the nearby towpath along the Delaware River. This enchanting linear path between the river and the feeder canal was once a bed for the Belvidere and Delaware Railroad; it is now part of the western branch of the extensive **D&R Canal State Park.**

The towpath is many, many miles long but you can, of course, commit to as much of it as you like, depending on your time and energy. (You

can always arrange to be picked up by car along the way.) With its romantic waterviews on both sides, it is among the most picturesque walks in the
region. On one side is the serene and straight canal, dotted with ducks and
geese; on the other is the dynamic and meandering Delaware.

If your starting point is Washington Crossing Park, you are about
halfway between Titusville (to the north) and Scudders Falls (to the south),
a distance of five to six miles each way. Choose whichever direction you
like; both are equally scenic and inviting. The path is nice and gentle, sur-
faced with loose gravel, making for easy walking. You'll often encounter
joggers and bikers. In places, the vegetation is quite sparse, exposing you
to the sun, a fact you should keep in mind on hot summer days. If you
decide to go as far as Scudder's Falls, you'll be rewarded with a view of this
beautiful sight. Along the way, enjoy the wildflowers—black-eyed Susans,
goldenrod, Queen Anne's lace, among many others. Aside from various
water birds, including blue herons, occasionally seen wading in the shallow water, you might see deer—or at least their tracks.

The canal towpath is open daily, year-round.

For a completely different kind of nature experience, one of pure
whimsy, surprise, and family fun, we take you to **Little Acres Corn Maze,** a
maze on a working farm. Here, amid five acres of cornfields fashioned
into an elaborate labyrinth of twists and turns, you can wander about in
trial-and-error mode, searching for the best exit route, while enjoying the
experience of being virtually enveloped by the very tall plants. Of course
you can't see the maze's intricate patterns—you would need to be in a heli-
copter for an aerial view—but you can visualize them as you meander
through the sinewy paths with their unexpected digressions.

Mazes are versions of the topiary, the ancient art of shaping plants
into living sculptures. Dating back at least to the Middle Ages, they were a
popular feature in the elegant garden designs of the Renaissance. But the
rustic corn maze is a modern concept. And, despite the fact that such
mazes last a relatively short time—only during the couple of months of
fall—and that they require intricate planning and maintenance, they seem
to be gaining visibility around the country.

Mazes are being designed in all sorts of fanciful ways these days. Some
feature realistic pictures—a farm scene or object, such as a barn, for

example. Others, like Little Acres Corn Maze, favor a swirl of geometric abstractions.

In addition to its main maze, Little Acres has a less challenging "kiddy-maze" that will appeal to younger children. Bear in mind that maze season is from Labor Day to Halloween, more or less, but phone the farm first to make sure. The farm also invites you to pick your own plum tomatoes and strawberries during May and June.

There is a fee for children over five and adults. Telephone: 609-737-6502.

IN THE VICINITY

Bowman's Hill State Wildflower Preserve, Washington Crossing State Park

After you have visited Washington Crossing Park on the New Jersey side of the Delaware, take a short drive across the river to this lovely preserve. Here you'll find an unusual medicinal trail walk that features plants that have real—or legendary—uses as medicines. Herb fanciers, as well as those interested in natural cures in general, will find this walk intriguing and informative.

The trail is about 620 feet long, which seems like nothing until you stop to examine each plant and read all sorts of interesting facts about it. Everything is carefully labeled and documented. You'll see mountain laurel (did you know that a long time ago Native Americans supposedly drank its juices to commit suicide?), mayapple and bloodroot (used for curing a sore throat in the old days), wild ginger, alumroot, fairywand, and witch hazel, among other varieties.

Bowman's Hill is known mostly for its magnificent wildflowers, a true delight in spring. If you have time after examining the medicinal plants, venture forth and explore. The preserve offers 100 acres of woodsy trails, meadows, ponds, an arboretum, and preserves for flowers and shrubs.

The preserve is located at 1635 River Rd., New Hope, PA. Telephone: 215-862-2924.

Bull's Island

The unusually picturesque Bull's Island (named after one Richard Bull, an original owner) was artificially created during the construction of the D&R canal. It is at this point that the Delaware River water enters the canal, becoming the "feeder" canal, which eventually meets the main canal at Trenton.

The long and slender island contains a natural area of some 24 acres, and what a pleasure they are! You can walk around at will, enjoying the views of the canal and the Delaware River, especially from a wonderful suspension bridge for pedestrians, which crosses the river to Pennsylvania. The scenery is quite densely wooded, with mostly Sycamore River birch, Elm silver maple, and one of the largest ostrich fern stands in the state, and you'll notice many vines climbing up the trees. Along the pebbled shore of the canal you might spot swans and ducks swimming around lazily. This is a popular area for canoeing, and both canoes and rowboats are available for renting.

If you are up to a longer hike, take any portion of a walking/biking trail that heads southeast along the canal. The trail, once the railroad bed for the Belvidere and Delaware Railroad, is some 17 miles long, but after 3 miles reaches the restored Prallsville Mill, the only historic multiple milling operation still in existence in New Jersey. The trail can be easily found on Bull's Island, as it starts next to the parking lot.

Bull's Island is located about 15 miles north of Washington Crossing Park on the New Jersey side of the Delaware. No fee.

24·
HAMILTON
TOWNSHIP

Grounds for Sculpture, Hamilton.

A Trio of Parks:
Sculpture, Flowers, and Bikeways

⚘ HOW TO GET THERE

Grounds for Sculpture

Take the New Jersey Turnpike to exit 7A, then I-195 west to to I-295 north, and to exit 65B, Sloan Avenue west. Go two-tenths of a mile and turn right at first traffic light. Follow signs for Grounds for Sculpture, turn left onto Klockner Road and turn right at first traffic light; go less than a mile and make the second left turn onto Sculptors Way, go two-tenths of a mile. Turn left onto Fairgrounds Road. You'll find Grounds for Sculpture down the road a bit, on your right, at 18 Fairgrounds Road in Hamilton.

Sayen Gardens

Take the New Jersey Turnpike to exit 7A, then I-195 west to Route 130 north. Go about one mile, turn left at the second traffic light to Route 33 west for another mile or so; bear right at the fork onto Nottingham Way. Turn right at the first traffic light (Mercer Road) and take your third left onto Hughes Drive. The gardens will be on your left.

Veterans Park

Take the New Jersey Turnpike to exit 7A, then Route 195 west to Yardsville/Hamilton Square exit; turn left at first light (Kuser Road). The park will be on your left about one mile down Kuser Road.

While exploring Mercer County, just east of Trenton and the Pennsylvania border, we discovered three particularly appealing parks, all in close proximity to one another. As a group they offer sculpture, gardens, and a vast parkland ideal for biking or long walks. And this outing becomes even more varied if you have time to visit the little-known historic site described later, which we chanced upon quite serendipitously.

🏵 **Grounds for Sculpture** is a relatively new (early 1990s) sculpture park and museum situated in Hamilton, on the former site of the New Jersey State Fair. The 22 acres of gently sloping terrain (once quite flat, like most of the region) are dotted with about 170 contemporary works set in an arboretum-like landscape of crab apples, dogwoods, weeping beeches, conifers, and other specimen trees. The grounds also contain a serene lotus pond, woodland marshes, a gazebo with observation deck (where you can have a snack and enjoy the view), and a picturesque iron arbor (a remnant of the past) with wisteria. Two large glass-walled museum buildings house the more intimate art works and changing exhibitions, and provide dramatic views of the outdoor installations.

The often bold, contemporary outdoor pieces, placed carefully in harmony with their natural surroundings, appear in grassy expanses, as well as amid the impeccably groomed flowering trees and shrubs. The works displayed are by emerging—as well as by established—artists, both American and international; they vary in size from monumental to very small indeed. Unlike the sculptures found on the nearby Princeton campus, these are likely to be by avant-garde artists whose names may not be familiar. Although some installations are permanent, there are temporary displays—usually three changing exhibits each year.

The park was created by the well-known sculptor J. Seward Johnson Jr., whose works are well represented elsewhere in the area (including in Princeton and in Veterans Park, below). His especially witty (and typically realistic) piece, "Dejeuner Déjà Vu," a take-off of Manet's seminal painting "Dejeuner sur l'Herbe," is on permanent display here. You'll find his lifelike figures seated quietly in the woods, on the edge of a small, secluded pond.

The park provides a striking setting for viewing art and nature together. On the grounds you'll find nice benches for resting, as well as an elegant restaurant with a terrace overlooking the scenic gardens.

Grounds for Sculpture is open daily (except Mondays and major holidays), year-round, from 10 A.M. to 9 P.M. Tours are available upon request, though you are welcome to take your own self-guided tour (ask for a brochure at the reception desk). Entrance fee. Telephone: 609-586-0616.

Sayen Gardens, in nearby Hamilton Square, is what you might describe as a "work in progress." Although most of it is now in place, parts of this 30-acre site are still being developed. It is always intriguing to see art works in progress—whether they are paintings, sculptures, or gardens— and Sayen Gardens is no exception. While observing existing colors, shapes, and textures, you wonder what the final outcome may be.

The property was once the country estate of Frederick Sayen, a successful rubber industrialist and avid gardener. From his travels to such distant lands as China, Japan, and England he brought back many unusual plants, including rare varieties of azaleas and rhododendrons. The gardens he designed to surround his English-style mansion were not completed at the time of his death in 1981; Hamilton Township bought the property from the family and has worked on the gardens ever since. (They were opened to the public in 1988.)

Over these years garden designers have been following Frederick Sayen's original plans—more or less. In order to add interest and promote better drainage, the once flat landscape has been contoured into one of gentle hills; a beautiful pond with arched bridge and surrounding gazebo and marble temple have been created; and new trails and botanic gardens continue to be developed.

From the moment you arrive, you are aware that Sayen Gardens are not only relatively new, but also meticulously kept. A pristine brick walk bordered by a profusion of impatiens and elephant ears (a continuing plant motif throughout the grounds) greets you at the entrance, leading to a most striking contemporary-style garden set upon a mound in front of the mansion. Its dramatic boulders (excavated when the landscape was contoured) form the centerpiece around which are groupings of exotic grasses and flowering plants combined in an eclectic, modern way. The overall arrangement is designed with an eye to colors, shapes, and textures. As you view it from a rustic woodchip path you'll note that, unlike traditional botanic gardens, nothing is labeled here; to identify the more unusual varieties you can consult one of the staff gardeners.

A number of paths through pine woods laced with wildflowers lead to other gardens. One takes you to a Japanese-style garden, complete with a pond and waterlilies, traditional arched bridge, and wooden gazebo. Tall grasses, iris, ferns, and hostas are found at water's edge. Another path leads to the Temple Gardens, where a small structure with marble columns and a lacy wrought-iron cupola is surrounded by a pretty lawn, bright flowers, ferns, and shrubs. The Native Azalea Garden is not to be missed in May, when it is a dazzling spectacle. (The annual Mother's Day azalea festival is a favorite event here.) And you can wander around through natural areas (some of which may be developed some day), enjoying the quiet woodlands.

Sayen Gardens are open daily, year-round, free of charge. Telephone: 609-890-3874.

Also located in Hamilton Square, **Veterans Park** provides quite a different experience from either of the preceding sites. This good-sized park (329 acres) is perfect for walkers and bikers, who can enjoy the miles of paved roadways and paths that wind around the green, well-kept grounds. (This is another meticulously maintained place.) Families with children, joggers, and bird watchers all come here to take advantage of the park's offerings. Park maps are available at the headquarters, and a large orientation map is posted near the children's playground, beside the parking lot.

Once a farmland, the park was completed in 1981. It is now filled with hundreds of trees (many of which have been donated by individuals through a special state and town program), as well as profusions of wildflowers, azaleas, and rhododendrons.

Walking in Veteran's Park is a real pleasure at all times of year. You can walk on a boardwalk to view a bog garden, or meander along a picturesque, winding creek in the woods, if you don't mind getting your feet a bit muddy now and again! Be sure to stop by the charming little flower garden located near the children's playground. This tiny (1.5-acre) oasis features a formal arrangement of flowers and shrubs surrounding a circular pool and fountain. Here, daffodils, canna lilies, foxgloves, and other colorful varieties proliferate each spring, along with glorious azaleas, hydrangeas, and viburnums.

Veterans Park is open daily, year-round, dawn to dusk, free of charge. Telephone: 609-581-4124.

IN THE VICINITY
Historic Walnford

We discovered this little-known site by chance, while exploring the region just south of Hamilton Township. A road sign pointing to "Historic Walnford," a place we had never heard of, caught our attention and, intrigued, we went to investigate.

Located off the beaten track at the end of a quiet country road next to a creek, Walnford is an idyllic 36-acre mill village listed on the National Register of Historic Places. (It is also a part of Cresswicks Creek Park, a 1,098-acre regional park.) Dating from colonial times, the picturesque site includes a grist mill on the banks of the creek and a charming group of cottages, sheds, and barns. Surrounding the structures (most of which have recently been restored) are grassy expanses and lovely old trees. You can walk around the grounds at will, enjoying the uncommercial and low-key ambience. Pick up the comprehensive walking guide, which describes in detail what and where everything is. Staff members are also around to answer questions.

The site has a long history dating from colonial times. Originally a plantation developed around the industrially important grist mill, the property was purchased by the Waln family shortly before the Revolutionary War. Under their guidance the farm expanded and thrived, producing flour, lumber, and other valuable commodities well into the late 1800s. In the 1980s the property was donated to the Monmouth County Park System and restoration of various structures began—including the Waln House, carriage house and corn barn, and, of course, the mill.

On our visit we saw an informative demonstration of corn milling, as well as exhibits of historic photos and archaeological artifacts found on the grounds. (We are told that additional programs relating to local history, nature, and milling are also offered.) Most of all, we enjoyed just walking, stopping at various spots, and taking in the pretty country views.

Historic Walnford is open daily, year-round, from 8 A.M. to 4:30 P.M. It is located on Walnford Road (off Route 539) in Crosswicks Creek Park, Upper Freehold Township. Telephone: 609-259-6275 or 732-842-4000.

25·
NORTH TIP OF
THE JERSEY
SHORE

Fort Hancock at Sandy Hook.

Exploring Sandy Hook: An Ocean Beach, a Holly Forest, and a Bay Island

HOW TO GET THERE

Sandy Hook (Visitor Center)

From the Garden State Parkway, take exit 117 to Route 36 east. Follow signs for Sandy Hook. The Visitor Center is located near Spermaceti Cove, at Area E. From here you can take the one-mile loop (Old Dune Trail), then move on to the other recommended sites.

Sandy Hook, part of the Gateway National Recreation area, is a slender, ribbonlike barrier beach peninsula at the northern tip of the New Jersey shore. Including some 1,665 acres of protected land, it has nearly seven miles of beachfront facing the Atlantic Ocean on one side and marshlands filled with migratory birds on the other, bay side. In between lies a long roadway with a few parking spots, a ranger station, and a visitor center. While part of the Hook has been developed by the New Jersey park system as a public beach, it is primarily a carefully controlled and somewhat restricted ecosystem of marshes and tidal pools supporting the thousands of migratory birds that come here to seek food and shelter.

Combining beaches, dunes, salt marshes, birds, woodlands, and even historic landmarks, Sandy Hook is an ideal spot for off-season walking and exploring: if you visit at a nonswimming time of year, you're likely to find few people, only occasional fishermen, hikers, or birders. (We do not recommend coming in summer, when beach traffic can become apocalyptic.) With its wonderful natural offerings—from dazzling ocean views to birds swooping in and out of the dune grass, to thousands of shells, driftwood, and other ocean "treasures" waiting to be collected—this is a perfect outing for families, including children. And the nice, flat terrain makes for pleasant and easy walking. Just remember to bring along a windbreaker (for chilly ocean breezes), comfortable shoes that can get wet, binoculars for birding, and a picnic (there are no food concessions off-season).

You can take any number of different walks, depending on your time and interests. Below are just a few options.

After picking up a trail guide and other park information at the Visitor Center (where you can also view a number of nature and historic exhibits), take the Old Dune Trail. This one-mile loop begins at the Center, opposite Spermaceti Cove (named for a beached whale long ago), then takes you briefly to the beach and back again. A free pamphlet (available at the Center) tells you which plants and animals you can expect to see. Watch for prickly

pear cactus, beach plum, and horseshoe crabs, among other natural curi-
osities. But beware of the very profuse poison ivy—stay on the trail! Along
the way you'll enter the edge of a unique 264-acre holly forest, much of
which is not accessible to the public and can only be seen on special tours.
Containing one of the greatest concentrations of the American holly in the
East, it has remarkably old specimens—some close to 200 years in age. Their
red berries are popular with much of the local bird population.

The South Beach Dune Trail, also a circular route, is a bit over a mile
long. Starting at the fishing beach it extends north, along the beach, where
you can watch endlessly the changing color of the ocean and the mesmerizing pattern of the waves rolling in. Take a moment to breathe in the
fresh salt air and to check out the usual flotsam that typically washes up on
shore. The trail moves inland through shrubs and thickets, into a mixed
forest of red cedars and black cherries, then back through another section
of the holly forest and a freshwater marsh.

Our favorite sites to explore on the bay side are Spermaceti Cove and
Plum Island, both wonderful spots for enjoying birds and water views.
Spermaceti Cove (across the road from the Visitor Center) is home to
some 267 species of birds, many of which—like the gannet, osprey, black
rail, and grebe—are endangered. With binoculars you might also spot warblers, sandpipers, marsh hawks, a great horned owl, woodpeckers, and
black ducks. Even with the naked eye you can see the many gulls and common waterbirds all around you. (Those who prefer more systematic bird
watching might opt for specialized tours organized by the New Jersey
Audubon Society.) If you're adventuresome you might wade out to Skele-
ton Hill Island, just off the cove, where you will likely find additional
marine specimens of interest.

Plum Island is a bit to the south, and is best reached from parking
area B. We recommend walking onto it at low tide, when it won't be necessary to do any wading. Because of its exposure to the wind, this little island
is a combination of amazing sand patterns, scrub vegetation, and wonderfully odd-shaped pieces of driftwood resembling exotic sculptures. From
here you'll find picturesque harbor views complete with boats and water
birds.

Before leaving Sandy Hook, you might visit one or both historic sites,
especially if you are interested in military history. (Because of its strategic

location, Sandy Hook has played an important role in defending and guiding ships through New York Harbor since the American Revolution.) Fort Hancock, on the northern end of the Hook, includes a lighthouse and museum, besides an extensive group of buildings relative to life on the fort, several of which are open to the public. But we found the other nearby attraction, Twin Lights, even more appealing. Constructed in 1828 as the Navesink Light Station, the site includes two rather ancient-looking light-houses high on a hill, some 256 feet above sea level. From the towers (which require climbing some 65 steps) you get, once again, wonderful views.

Sandy Hook is open to the public year-round. The Visitor Center is open daily from 10 A.M. to 5 P.M. To arrange for bird watching tours sponsored by the New Jersey Audubon Society, call 908-872-0115. Parking fees along the beach apply only during the summer. Telephone: 732-872-5970.

IN THE VICINITY
Poricy Park

Poricy, located on Oak Hill Road in Middletown, is an inviting park of marshes, deep woods, fields of wildflowers, and a pond filled with water birds. What makes it more than just another pleasant outdoor family spot is that it lies in an area where many fossils have been uncovered. Millions of years ago the site was a shallow ocean containing sea creatures; in Poricy Brook you can still dig for fossils in an ancient bed some 65 million years old. Although dinosaur remains have been found here—a fact that is certain to intrigue many a child—more common are snails, sea urchins, and sponges. (You are allowed to take home whatever treasure you might find.)

The park also offers nice walking trails (easy enough for children in tow), a visitor center with fossil and hands-on exhibits, a colonial farm-house and barn, and quite a variety of wildlife—including occasional hawks.

Poricy Park is open year-round, from dawn to dusk; there is no entrance fee. Telephone for Visitor Center hours: 732-842-5966.

Huber Woods

This 265-acre hardwood forest off Brown's Dock Road in Navesink over-looking the Navesink River surrounds a Swiss-style farm that once belonged to the Huber family. (Its manor house is now used for nature displays.) The surrounding woodlands feature oaks, tulips, beeches, and poplars, and an especially dark and mysterious grove of Norwegian spruce. The walking trails are pleasant and easy, taking you through gently sloping terrain as you meander through fields and woods. Telephone: 732-872-2670.

26·
EASTERN MONMOUTH COUNTY

Off the North Jersey Shore: A Salt Marsh, an Arboretum, a Dogwood Trail, and a Garden with a Past

Cheesequake State Park.

🌿 HOW TO GET THERE

Cheesequake State Park

Take the Garden State Parkway to exit 120 and follow signs to the park; go past the park office and leave your car in a small area on the left, just beyond.

Holmdel Park and Arboretum

From Holmdel, take Route 520 to Holmdel Road for about two miles; go east on Roberts Road, turn left at Longstreet Road, and follow signs to Holmdel Park.

Tatum Park

Take the Garden State Parkway to exit 114 onto Red Hill Road (from Parkway North turn right, from Parkway South turn left), continue for one mile to the Red Hill Activity Center entrance.

Deep Cut Gardens

Located at 352 Red Hill Road in Middletown, directly across the street from Tatum Park, just over a mile east of exit 114 from the Garden State Parkway.

This diverse coastal plain combines marshes, open fields, pine and hardwood forests, swampy terrain, and, in places, the sandy soil you expect to see near the ocean. In fact, you are quite close to the upper reaches of the shore, and just north of the Pine Barrens.

🦌 **Cheesequake State Park** near Raritan Bay offers hiking or walking trails through several different habitats, making it an ideal spot in which to enjoy a wide variety of plants and wildlife.

The 1,274-acre park, whose unusual sounding name was given by the Leni-Lenape Indians (who fished and hunted here as early as 3000 B.C.), was an area once mined for its fine clay. It was opened as a public park in 1940 and has since offered fishing and swimming, camping, picnicking, and—especially of interest to us—hiking on some very scenic trails.

There are three main hiking trails, all clearly identified in a brochure available at the entrance. On our last visit we chose the yellow trail, a relatively short (about 30 minutes of walking) but nice loop that takes you through beautiful woodlands uphill, then back down through a salt marsh to a lake (Hooks Creek Lake). We saw swamp azalea, mountain laurel, and many fine old trees—beech, birch, oaks, and white pine—and were told this is one of New Jersey's premier spots to view pink lady's slipper (in springtime). Throughout the park, and especially around the marsh, are a wide number of birds (some 186 species have been seen).

The park is open daily year-round; the interpretive center (where you can also make arrangements for a guide) is open from Wednesday through Sunday. There is a parking fee from Memorial Day weekend through Labor Day. Telephone: 908-566-2161.

For a very different kind of experience, try **Holmdel Park and Arboretum,** a delightfully rustic county park. In addition to the expected park amenities—walking trails, playing fields, and picnic areas—the park features a 300-year-old "living-history" farm (a popular destination for schoolchildren during the week) and a marvelous arboretum.

Longstreet Farmhouse, a 300-year-old farm set near a picturesque pond with woods beyond, has been recently restored to its late Victorian period. Here you can wander about and get a taste of nineteenth-century farm life, including costumed personnel.

The much quieter hillside arboretum offers a collection of ornamental trees and shrubs that have been grouped according to color of bloom. Most are tagged for easy identification. The red group, set along both sides of the pond, features crab apples, large weeping cherries, flowering plums, and hawthorns, a dazzling sight especially in spring; a blue collection contains dwarf conifers and larger evergrees that come in subtle gradations of blue and green and even gold; other collections include a dark green pine grouping, light green spruces, purple rhododendrons, and even "gray" sections. The most unusual arrangement is undoubtedly the Synoptic Garden, a group of shrubs and trees planted in—of all things—alphabetical order!

The 20-acre arboretum was established in 1963 for the study and enjoyment of its many plants, all native to the region. You can wander about at will and take in the sights and delicate fragrances that perfume the air. If you wish to walk farther, there are nearby nature trails through oak, beech, and hickory woods.

The arboretum is open all year, from 8 A.M. to dusk, and there is no entrance fee. Telephone: 732-431-7903 or 732-842-4000.

Set within 368 acres of open meadows, rolling hills, and woodsy trails, **Tatum Park** is the perfect spot for a nice walk, year-round. It offers five or six trails varying in length (from a half-mile loop to a 2.5-mile trail), some even for bikers and equestrians, as well as walkers. A brochure with map (available at the trailheads and the parking area) directs you to a holly trail, where you walk through a spectacular grove of hollies; a meadow trail through fields, and an uphill walk on an old farm road, among other areas. We especially liked the Dogwood Hollow Trail, a peaceful one-mile loop into woodlands of enchanting flowering dogwoods—try it in May.

The park is open all year, every day, from 8 A.M. to sunset and is free of charge. Telephone: 732-842-4000.

Deep Cut Gardens, directly across the street, have a story with a mysterious past. The site, once farmland, became in 1935 the property of the infamous Mafia boss Vito Genovese. Not surprisingly, he was a big spender: his Italian stone masons built extensive walls (the festoonlike stone walls surrounding the property are quite unusual), ornamental pools, and even a replica of Mount Vesuvius. The gardens surrounding the house featured rare plants and trees, among them the magnificent gnarled hemlocks that still overlook the terrace gardens. In 1937 Genovese suddenly left for Italy when he was being investigated by the authorities, and during his absence a mysterious fire destroyed the mansion; it is not known who was responsible so the case remains unsolved to this day. After the war (and a few additional scandals), the property was taken over by new owners, who created greenhouses and many of the gardens that still exist today. In 1977 it became part of the county park system and has been enjoyed by the public ever since.

The gardens on these 53 acres are arranged in an informal way, with one flowing into the next, making this a very pleasant place in which to walk. Some are hillside gardens, including a shade garden (with a canopy of dogwood, tulip, cedar, and poplar trees), an azalea and rhododendron walk, a rockery, and a small orchard. There are hummingbird and butterfly gardens filled with brilliant flowers and shrubs to attract those species, a wisteria-covered pergola, a lily pond filled with a brightly colored Koi, a meadow with wildflowers, and a variety of demonstration gardens for new gardeners. Plans are being made for a parterre with perennial flowers.

Deep Cut offers something for the visitor at all times of the year. A greenhouse contains orchids, succulents, and other plants for year-round enjoyment. In June and September there are impressive displays of roses (those in the know consider them quite special, and they have won prestigious awards over the years), and with May come thousands of brightly colored tulips.

Deep Cut Gardens are open daily, year-round, from 8 A.M. to dusk. The park is free of charge. Telephone: 732-671-6050.

IN THE VICINITY

Hartshorne Woods Park

From Atlantic Highlands go east on Route 36, follow signs for "Scenic Road;" take Navesink Avenue for half a mile to park entrance.

This scenic 736-acre park overlooking the Navesink River contains miles of trails not only for hikers, but also for mountain bikers, equestrians, and cross-country skiers. (Trails are marked according to their intended use.) The area is covered with dense woodlands and is surprisingly hilly, making some of the trails fairly steep. One of the most beautiful paths is the Laurel Ridge Trail, which reaches a very scenic overlook with views of the river. Along the way you'll find groups of hollies, sassafras, hickories, and tulip trees, among the many varieties. Watch for squirrels, deer, and occasional (especially on weekends) mountain bikes.

The park is open daily, year-round. Telephone: 732-842-4000.

Thompson Park: Lambertus C. Bobbink Memorial Rose Garden

Surrounded by 665 acres of playing fields, a lake, fitness trails, and tennis courts, lies this surprisingly quiet rose garden.

Created in the 1970s in memory of the dean of American rosarians, it displays thousands of award-winning roses. The more than 1,500 plants are carefully labeled and documented. For those wishing more information, there is a flyer indicating the latest plant listings with accompanying descriptions. On this appealing site are flowerbeds arranged in unusual shapes, rounded gazebos with climbing roses, and wonderfully vibrant colors.

Thompson Park and the rose garden are open daily from 8 A.M. to dusk. Of course, the best time to enjoy roses is from May to September. The park is located at 805 Newman Springs Road, Lincroft. Telephone: 732-842-4000.

27·
FREEHOLD
REGION

Allaire Village.

*A Battlefield, a Reservoir Loop,
a Meadow Walk on a Rail Trail,
and an Abandoned Village*

✿ HOW TO GET THERE

Monmouth Battlefield

Take exit 123 off the Garden State Parkway, to Route 9 south, to Hemlock Road. Follow signs.

Manasquan Reservoir

Take Route 9 south to Georgia Tavern Road to Windeler Road; turn right.

Freehold and Jamesburg Rail Trail

Take exit 98 off the Garden State Parkway to Route 34 south, right at first light onto Allenwood Road; right on Atlantic Avenue, left onto Hospital Road. Trail entrance is on your right at two-tenths of a mile.

Allaire Deserted Village

Take exit 98 off the Garden State Parkway to Route 34 south, right onto Allenwood Road. Follow signs to Allaire State Park.

✿ This part of New Jersey features pretty, rolling countryside with meadows and lakes and ideal walking or biking terrain. This lovely area is wonderfully open for walking, with wide vistas all around at **Monmouth Battlefield,** the site of a major 1778 battle between the Continental forces of General George Washington and the British under General Henry Clinton. The 2,000-acre site still looks just as it must have looked more than 200 years ago, with its extensive views and evocative ambience. There are 25 miles of trails through fields, woods, and marshes, and you'll particularly like the gentle hills dotted with eighteenth-century hedgerows. It was here that Washington attacked the British as they were swinging east from Philadelphia, and here too that "Molly Pitcher" carried water to the troops and then took charge of her husband's cannon to help out.

As historic sites go, this one is pleasantly uncommercial. You can discover as much information as you wish concerning the largest and most dramatic—though inconclusive—battle of the Revolutionary War at the excellent museum. This fully operational Visitor Center has electronic and historical displays aplenty, and there are annual reenactments in June. But just a walk over these vast grounds gives an undeniable sense of history, either in a guided tour or on your own. There are also riding trails and picnic spots here.

The park is open year-round. Admission is free. Telephone: 732-462-9616.

🌿 Not far away, **Manasquan Reservoir** is a decided change of pace. This very large, tranquil body of water is a major summer destination for boaters and swimmers, so we recommend visiting for walks or bike rides off-season. We found it particularly inviting on a beautiful autumn day when the trees that surround the reservoir were brilliantly colored. There is a five-mile perimeter trail—a loop—around the entire lake, with water views, squawking waterfowl, and lovely light filtering through the trees. In winter you might see occasional skaters on the ice. Walking is pleasant here on an unpaved but flat path, and bird watching is excellent.

The trails are open year-round. There is a fee for parking in summer only. Telephone: 732-842-4000.

🌿 In the same region you'll find a most unusual walk: the **Freehold and Jamesburg Rail Trail.** While this old secondary line of Penn-Central's Freehold railroad track can be entered from either Allenwood or Farmingdale, we recommend beginning your walk in Allenwood, just near Allaire State Park (our next destination). This 4.5-mile railroad track, which begins in a meadow, accommodated agricultural trains in the 1800s. Today it is a pleasant hiking route—no tracks in sight—passing by fields and farms, a golf course, and occasional wooded areas. Parts of it reminded us of English countryside walks through farmers' fields and rights-of-way. It ends up in deep woods, near Farmingdale. (As this is not a loop walk, figure your distances accordingly.)

🌿 One of the most picturesque village walks we know is through the **Allaire Deserted Village.** Once a bustling iron forge center, known in 1763 as the Williamsburg Forge, it became known as Allaire when in 1822 Benjamin Howell and James Allaire opened their bog iron production on the site. Employing some 400 people, the bog iron ore, which was produced by decaying vegetation, was smelted and cast into pots and pans, pipes and stoves, and numerous other iron items. By the mid-nineteenth century, however, better-quality iron was being produced elsewhere, and the forge—and indeed the whole village—was abandoned.

A walk through the village today is quite an extraordinary experience. The winding roadway takes you past small houses, the school, the general store, the old New England-style meeting house, the bakery, the sawmill—

and much, much more, all tastefully restored and many buildings resoundingly empty. There are streams and little bridges, fields, and several nice nature trails. The entire environment recreates the ambience of a small rural settlement of long ago. It is curiously still and provides a dreamlike atmosphere for your walk.

The deserted village is just part of the larger state park, which has additional nature walks and other facilities. The park is officially open from May to Labor Day with a parking fee. But you can visit the village at any time except during January and February. There are tours available too, and in season there is a steam train ride on the Pine Creek Railroad for the kids. Telephone: 732-938-2253.

 IN THE VICINITY

Turkey Swamp

Georgia Road in Freehold Township. This 17-acre lake is home to the most unbelievable number of waterfowl. A walk here might include a one-mile fitness trail or bird and wildlife watching in a natural Pine Barrens region. Telephone: 732-462-7286.

Battleview Orchards

Just next to Monmouth Battlefield on Wemrock Road off Route 33 is this extensive orchard—100 acres of neat rows of apple, peach, and cherry trees, as well as thousands of pumpkins. Pick your own, or wander about at will in season. If you've never walked in an orchard, you'll find it is a particular pleasure; you feel a bit like a chess piece on a vast, orderly board. There is also a massive retail shed. Phone for precise times to walk in the orchard. Telephone: 732-462-0970.

Owl Haven

Located on Route 522 in Tennent (on Monmouth Battlefield property), Owl Haven is run by the New Jersey Audubon Society, and it lives up to its name. You can visit in the afternoons and walk through the fields and woods here, hoping to spot these rare creatures outdoors. If you have no luck, some are also kept indoors. There are also many other birds, and butterflies too. Telephone: 732-780-7007.

28 ·
LAKEWOOD
AREA

Georgian Court College campus.

Lakeside Pleasures:
Biking and Hiking Lakeside Loops
and a Georgian Campus

ॐ HOW TO GET THERE

Lake Shenandoah Park

From the Garden State Parkway, take exit 91 (Route 549) south to Route 88 and go west. The entrance to Lake Shenandoah Park is about two miles farther west, on your left.

Ocean County Park

The entrance is almost directly across the street (Route 88) from Lake Shenandoah.

Lake Carasaljo

From Route 88, continue west to traffic light at intersection with Route 9. Turn left on Route 9 for one block and you'll see the lake on your right. To park at one of many entrance points for the walking loop, turn right on North Lake Drive.

Georgian Court College

The entrance to the campus is just off North Lake Drive, at 900 Lakewood Avenue, a short block from Lake Carasaljo.

Lakewood is blessed with several large and glistening bodies of water, and, fortunately, each is easily accessible. You will have your choice of scenery, depending on whether you choose to make your way around the pristine, woodsy Lake Shenandoah, the (slightly) more urban Lake Carasaljo, the pretty fishing lakes of Ocean County Park, or the wonders of a sculpture-filled campus with its own lagoon. Perhaps you will explore all of them, for this is a particularly attractive region of the state.

ॐ **Lake Shenandoah Park** provides a two-mile loop—our idea of a perfect distance for a nice brisk walk. The path is mostly sandy, though occasionally asphalt. It winds around this very pretty lake, just above the water level, and you can enjoy both the scenery (there are particularly good water views after the leaves have fallen) and the cries of waterfowl. The park encompasses about 143 acres; the lake itself covers 50 of them. There are many species of fish, more than 25; some are natural to the lake and others are kept stocked. The lake is actually known for its herring, and yes, fishing is allowed. After you've walked around the lake you'll find a nice shaded picnic area and even a tiny bait and coffee shop awaiting you.

Lake Shenandoah Park, which is open year-round, is one of Ocean County's parks. For information telephone the Park Department at 732-506-9090, ext. 237, or 877-OC PARKS.

❀ Just across the road and a short way west is the entrance to the unusually nice **Ocean County Park.** Your first notice of it will be the rows of huge hemlocks lining the perimeter of the park. With their beautiful high branches and the cleared, needle-covered ground below, they are an inviting sight. This lovely area of northern Ocean County was once John D. Rockefeller's summer home.

When you enter the park you'll find a great variety of recreational choices, from tennis courts to beaches and fishing areas (including Lake Fishigan just for junior fishermen). There are several small lakes, including one with a sandy beach. Of particular interest to us, of course, were the pretty walking trails that crisscross the 323-acre area. There are unusually nice forested areas—including some 150 types of trees originally planted in the twenties and thirties for Mr. Rockefeller. With its paved pathways, this is a particularly good park for biking or, in winter, for delicious cross-country skiing. But there are also dirt trails into the wooded areas, and we recommend these for those who prefer more solitude on their walks.

Ocean County Park is open year-round. For information, call the Park Office at 732-506-9090, ext. 237.

❀ The town of Lakewood borders the long, narrow **Lake Carasaljo.** This picturesque body of water is surrounded by nice playgrounds, occasional houses, and attractive village views. It is intersected by a bridge. There are entrance points for the lakeside walkway at several different points. If you prefer your lakeside walks with fewer trees and more civilization to look at, you will like this loop.

❀ For a complete change of view and ambience, visit **Georgian Court College.** This is truly a delightful college campus, and it invites visitors, though be sure to check in at the entrance gate. Its very name suggests an eighteenth-century setting in England, and, in fact, it reminds the walker of a great British estate with its stately home, arched hedges, lagoon, and fine marble statuary. Despite an occasional glimpse of the thousand students who attend college here, you will feel as though you are wandering around a great European manor's grounds (or perhaps are in a scene from *Masterpiece Theater*).

Enclosed by high walls, the campus is a glamorous compilation of formal gardens and fine statues. It was once the home of the financier and railroad magnate George Jay Gould. When Gould purchased 175 acres in 1896, he set about building a mansion (still magnificent) and having gardens designed that equaled its splendor and matched its Georgian-era architecture. In the Italian and classical style, you'll find an elliptical formal garden comprised of sixteen separate flowerbeds bordered by boxwood. There are also Japanese gardens, with a teahouse and arched wooden bridge. In the center of the campus is a great allée of trees and classical marble sculpture that is well worth a walk from one end to the other. The pièce de résistance is the great Apollo fountain designed by American sculptor John Massey Rhind; its marble horses plunge dramatically from the waters of the lagoon. A flight of steps will take you to the lake itself and a sunken garden. For harmonious design, this campus can rival any you may have visited.

Georgian Court College is open during daytime hours. Call for information before you visit: 732-364-2200.

29·
TOMS RIVER
REGION

Bay Head.

Coastal Pleasures:
Islands, Oceanside, Bayside, Bogside

 **HOW TO GET THERE**

Island Beach State Park

From the Garden Sate Parkway, take exit 82A to Route 37 east. Continue across bridge, turn right on Route 35 to the park.

Cattus Island

From Route 37 in Toms River, go north on Fischer Boulevard to Cattus Island Road on your right. You can leave your car inside the park at the end of the road.

Ocean County College's Sambol-Citta Arboretum

From Cattus Island, return to Fischer Boulevard and continue north to its end. Turn left on Hooper Avenue (Route 549) for a short distance; entrance to college campus is on your right. Follow college drive to parking lot 2A; walk back to arboretum entrance just before lot.

Island Beach is one of the few undeveloped barrier beaches on the North Atlantic coast. The southern section of the narrow peninsula was saved as parkland only in 1959. Thank goodness for the foresight of the state, which stepped in when the National Park Service failed to raise the money. And what a glorious place this is! (We should warn you that we are not the only visitors to find it a wonderful place to walk and swim and fish and breathe the ocean air. We recommend visiting **Island Beach State Park** in the off-season—for over a million visitors come during the summertime.)

The narrow spit of land—from Bay Head in the north to the southern tip at Island Beach State Park—offers exactly what nature intended for a barrier island: dunes, dune vegetation, sea birds, beach, shells, fish—and absolutely no commercial development. There is an environmental center and a parking area here and there, but essentially it is a pristine landscape that beckons to walkers or bikers alike. If you are a seaside lover who relishes the salt smell and continuous roar of the ocean, you'll love this place.

There are several different walks you may take here. Over four miles of trails have been laid out, some of them on boardwalks through the sand—a very pleasant way to hike through sand dunes. We suggest that you begin at the headquarters where you may pick up a clearly marked map showing the different types of walks, as well as material on birding or vegetation. (Be sure to ask for the history brochure—the island has a long and fascinating past.) Keep in mind that since this is a very narrow spit of land, walks can go either to the oceanside or the bayside from the center roadway that bisects the length of the island. There is a striking difference between the calm and inviting bayside, where beach plum trees and gnarled driftwood lie along a gentle sandy shore with shallow water, and the magnificent Atlantic with its roaring surf and stupendous beach of fine white sand.

Recommended walks here include one known as A-7 on a boardwalk to both bay and ocean through holly, bayberry, dune grass (which anchors the sand), and shortened trees (the effect of salt spray). Another suggested outing is Spizzle Creek, where wading birds and ospreys abound. Walk A-13 takes you through a freshwater wetland where cranberries grow. Walks are generally less than one mile long. Be careful not to disturb any part of nature here. And breathe deeply—this is some of the best air in the state of New Jersey.

Island Beach State Park is open daily year-round. There is a charge (higher in season). There are numerous events for children and adults, and tours are available. Telephone: 732-793-0506.

Cattus Island is a surprise; you come upon it suddenly in a woefully commercial region of Toms River, drive down the long path through lovely tall pines, and leave your car. Suddenly you find yourself in a county park that is surely one of the most unusual landscapes in all the state. For on a nice boardwalk you traverse a world of salt marsh and bogs and forested wetlands that feels a million miles from where you were ten minutes before. Cattus Island covers five hundred acres on a peninsula—all the way to Barnegat Bay. (It is called an island because at certain tides it is cut off from the mainland.)

This is a wetland environment that seems quite out of this world, for the strange reeds (called phragmites) that border the walkway are at least eight feet tall and dwarf us as we go among them. Birds abound; you can see them darting among the reeds, and can hear them singing in the silence of this picturesque landscape. Great expanses of bogs and wetland vegetation stretch out before you at the end of one boardwalk; you can easily imagine the salt marshes being used by patriots and privateers to bring in and off-load British ships during the Revolutionary War. There are white cedar swamps, freshwater bogs, pine oak forests, brackish water estuaries, and the saltwater bay. You'll find over 300 different types of vegetation, including hollies, grasses, swamp azalea, sand myrtle, and the wonderful phragmites.

Begin your outing at the Cooper Environmental Center, where you can pick up a map or arrange for a tour. There are six miles of trails, many open to bicycles, wheelchairs, and strollers as well as walkers. Choose your outing by the type of environment you most enjoy walking through; the guides at headquarters will help. We recommend the boardwalk (red trail) into the reeds, for a truly unusual walk. We enjoyed this walk in spring when the air was fresh and there were no bugs; in mosquito season be sure to use your bug spray.

Cattus Island is open from 8 A.M. to sunset daily. There is no charge. Telephone: 732-270-6960.

The **Arboretum at Ocean County College,** a large, modernistic campus not far away from Cattus Island, is entirely different in ambience. Here you'll find a well-maintained, beautifully laid-out tree garden, for that is essentially what it is. There are no labels here, but there are lovely paths through stands of Norway spruce, lilacs, dogwood, mountain laurel, azaleas in an Azalea Grove, and ferns in a Fern Cobble. The brick paths are designed in a series of geometrical circles, and inviting wooden benches are provided here and there. There is a pond with a holly grove nearby, and a variety of habitats. The arboretum has a 1.5-mile nature trail alongside leading to a hardwood swamp. Birdwatchers will enjoy this outing too.

The arboretum, a gift of Richard S. Sambol and Joseph A. Citta, was designed to stimulate environmental awareness in the college community and to be a refuge both for people and for birds. These ten acres are a lovely oasis of quiet and in springtime are particularly nice for a walk. The arboretum is open daily, dawn to dusk, year-round. Free. Telephone: 732-255-4000.

30·
THE PINE
BARRENS

Double Trouble State Park.

Cranberry Bogs in the Pine Barrens:
Double Trouble State Park
and Lebanon State Forest

 HOW TO GET THERE

Double Trouble State Park

From the Garden State Parkway, take exit 80. Turn left (south) onto Double Trouble Road and go to the end of the road (about three miles). The park entrance is located directly in front of you, at the intersection with Pinewald-Keswick Road. Cranberry Village is just beyond the entrance.

Lebanon State Forest (main entrance and Visitor Center)

Take exit 67 off the Garden State Parkway to Route 554 west, to Route 72. The entrance is one mile east of the intersection with Route 70, on your right. Stop at the Visitor Center for maps and other information.

Whitesbog Village (Lebanon State Forest)

Take Route 70 east from its intersection with Route 72; go left on Route 530. Follow signs to the entrance (on your right).

Pakim Pond (Lebanon State Forest)

Continue east on Route 72 to entrance to Pakim Pond within the park.

The Pine Barrens is one of the greatest expanses of wilderness in the Northeast, including more than one million acres of dense forests, swamps, rivers, and pitch pine lowlands. (See Chapter 32 for more hikes in the Pine Barrens.) A visit to the following two parks within this vast region comes with a double surprise: the fact that there is still so much virtually undeveloped land not far from the bustling shore, and the fact that in both parks there is, of all things, an abandoned cranberry village. Yes, New Jersey was—and still is—an important cranberry-producing state (it's third after Massachusetts and Wisconsin), a statistic that may not be widely known. And much of this activity took place on these very sites. So, if you like walks combining history with nature, head for **Double Trouble State Park** and **Lebanon State Forest**, where you can experience the beauty of the Pine Barrens (without committing to an arduous hike), along with a walk through historic villages.

The curious name "Double Trouble," which began with the cranberry industry, may have one of two origins: a certain Thomas Potter said those words in disgust after heavy rains washed out the dam twice; or the words were shouted out by workmen after discovering two leaks in the dam, presumably caused by gnawing beavers.

Cranberry farming was particularly suited to this area of cedar forests and flowing streams; as trees were cut down, cleared swamplands were planted with cranberry vines. By the early part of the twentieth century, the cranberry industry was thriving here under the Double Trouble Cranberry Company, and the village was in full operation. Until the 1960s, when farming demands and methods began to change, some of the state's largest harvests came from these bogs. Today only a few of the remaining bogs are harvested under special lease arrangements with local growers.

The Double Trouble Historic District, as the abandoned village and its immediate surroundings are known, is situated on high ground between two bogs (one is now dry) and provides you with a view of what a cranberry production community was like. Before exploring the village (it makes more sense to do that first, and then take your nature walk), stop at the small office on the right and pick up a map that identifies each building (13 are listed), as well as a detailed nature trail guide. The village is very rustic and the ambience refreshingly uncommercial—as of now, anyway, there is no entrance fee and nothing at all to buy. You can just wander about at your own pace, enjoying this small settlement as it more or less was, on the dirt road along the creek. Among the building highlights are the 1890 schoolhouse (the oldest remaining structure), the workers' cottages (usually, two families lived in one small hut), the "newer" sawmill next to the creek (an eighteenth-century sawmill is being restored), and the imposing sorting and packing house.

Just below the packing house you'll see the beginning of the well marked 1.5-mile nature trail. This very picturesque sandy trail takes you on a loop along a series of cranberry bogs (now under water or under marshy growth), which you can easily identify with your nature guide. Fresh, clean water is everywhere, some areas deep, others quite shallow, all carefully damned and controlled. (Fishing is allowed in some areas.) If you visit in late September or early October you might see workers actually harvesting the cranberries. When shaken from the vine, the berries float to the water surface, then are gathered by machines. During the winter months the bogs are flooded to protect the plants from the bitter cold.

Also well documented in the guide is the Pine Barrens vegetation you will see along the way, from the pitch pine and scrub oak, to the red "swamp" maple, Atlantic white cedar (ideal for making boats and shingles), sweet bay magnolia, and the prolific mountain laurel. You'll notice quite a number of dead trees (where migratory birds like to nest), drowned from too much water.

Double Trouble State Park is open daily, year-round, from dawn to dusk. There is no entrance fee. Telephone: 732-341-6662.

🐾 Within the much larger Lebanon State Forest, the cranberry industry is represented by another intriguing place, **Whitesbog Village.** The village, listed as both a National and State Historic Site, is mostly intact, with many of its quaint old buildings from the early 1900s still standing. Surrounding it are the remains of what was once one of the largest cranberry and blueberry farms in all of New Jersey, originally owned by the White family.

Before starting off, be sure to stop at the Company Store or the kiosk on the edge of town, where maps and self guides are usually available. After poking around the village (part of which is being restored), you can take two walking trails—the Old Bog Nature Trail (a short one through the edge of an old abandoned bog) and the Whitesbog Village Tree Trail (where you'll see a good sampling of tree varieties found in the area). If you're up for a rare adventure, we recommend the five-mile self driving tour that loops from the village through the nearby cranberry bogs, blueberry fields, and pine forests and across dams and canals on a network of narrow sandy roads. The fascinating vistas range from "villagy" to woodsy to vast moonscape-like panoramas with dead tree stumps in water, sand flats, and bright orange sand paths. You'll find the ambience surprisingly desolate—we met not a soul—but truly mesmerizing.

Whitesbog Village is always open, year-round. Free of charge. For information, call the Whitesbog Preservation Trust Office at 609-893-4646.

🐾 The cranberry theme continues at **Pakim Pond.** Cranberry bogs existed here, too, as they did in much of the region, and the pond was once a reservoir used to store water for the fall flooding of a nearby bog (now a swamp). The word "pakim" is, in fact, a Leni-Lenape Indian term for "cranberry."

A one-mile nature trail, which loops around the pond and swamp, is a pleasant, easy, woodsy walk on beds of soft pine needles. A self-guiding tour (available at the park office) notes several points of interest where you can spot many varieties of plants and animals, from carpenter frogs, red-bellied turtles, raccoons, foxes, oppossums, water snakes, and myriad birds, to carnivorous plants, arrowhead plants (once used by Native Americans), and, yes, wild cranberries. Cedars, maples, and pitch pines abound in these deep woods. Swimmers can enjoy the pond in season, as can campers (note several rustic wood cabins picturesquely situated at water's edge).

Pakim Pond is open to walkers year-round, free of charge. For information call the main office at Lebanon State Forest: 609-726-1191.

IN THE VICINITY
Wells Mills County Park

From Lebanon State Forest take Route 72 (east), turn left onto Route 532 and continue for about three miles; the park entrance will be on your right.

This delightfully unspoiled park includes 16 miles of marked hiking trails through woods and swamps and freshwater bogs, with soft moss underfoot. At the center of the 900-acre site is a clear lake which you can circle on foot—even crossing a dam at one point. (During colonial times the first of two sawmills was built here to accommodate the region's growing need for lumber.) There is also an impressive Nature Center, which offers exhibits and a variety of programs; from its observation deck you can enjoy a spectacular view of the surrounding Pine Barrens.

Wells Mills County Park is open year-round; the Nature Center's hours are 10 A.M. to 4 P.M. daily. Telephone: 609-971-3085.

31·
PEMBERTON
REGION

Trillium in early spring.

Nature's Color: A Boardwalk through Wooded Wetlands, a Great Rail Trail, a Waterside Ravine, and a Giant Corn Maze

❧ HOW TO GET THERE

Dot and Brooks Evert Memorial Nature Trail

From the New Jersey Turnpike, exit 7, take Route 206, then Route 530 east to Pemberton. At the intersection of Route 530 and Magnolia Road turn right. Make an immediate right onto Scrapetown Road, which will become Stockton's Bridge Road. Turn left at its end onto Ong's Hat Road. You'll find the trail entrance on your left after half a mile.

Pemberton Rail Trail

Take Route 206 as above to Route 530, following signs into the village of Pemberton. You'll find the North Pemberton Railroad Station (now a museum), where you can access the rail trail, at the end of the main street of town at 3 Fort Dix Road.

Smithville County Park

From the New Jersey Turnpike, exit 7, take Route 206 south to Route 38 (which to the east is called 530). Go west on Route 38 for about one-half mile to a right turn on Smithville-Jacksonville Road. Go north on this road for less than one mile, until you come to the historic town of Smithville and the County Park on your left. There are several entrances and parking areas, all of which lead to unusual sights. The first is on your left just after the historic church, the second across the bridge, also on your left, and the third is beyond the historic house of Hezekial Smith.

Bauma's Farm Corn Maze

From Route 206 north of Pemberton (west of Jobstown), turn west on Route 670. You'll find the Farmer's Market and maze on your right on the Jacksonville-Burlington Road (Route 670).

This rural region of the state—just to the west of the Pine Barrens—is filled with blueberry farms and lovely woods, flat sandy paths, and a few historic villages, including Pemberton, tucked in here and there. Its natural beauties are particularly evident in fall, when the black gums turn lovely shades of scarlet, and swamp maples, willow oak, pitch pine, and sassafras add to the autumn colors. Flat expanses of farmland and an occasional small, rushing river make this an especially nice region for a walk.

Pemberton is a very old community whose tiny, bright storefronts are close upon the street like those of so many eighteenth-century villages. Its downtown has been, for the most part, undisturbed, and you'll enjoy a walk around it—both via the main street and on the recently opened rail trail. The fact that there are terrific hiking areas so close by (with the Pine Barrens within easy reach) makes it a good destination for a day's outing.

🐝 Walking on the **Dot and Brooks Evert Memorial Nature Trail** is most unusual, because it is almost entirely on a boardwalk over wetlands and under a canopy of great trees. Under the aegis of the New Jersey Conservation Foundation, this well-kept trail is a delight. The Everts, for whom the site is named, were strong conservationists and devoted their energies to preserving this unusual wetland environment on the edge of the Pine Barrens. Although it encompasses only 170 acres, with a 1.5-mile trail looping through it, you'll feel far away from civilization. It is divided by a marvelously named stream, Stop-the-Jade Run, and the area is in fact almost entirely wet.

For a good ecological description of this unusual site, pick up—and return—a booklet from the box at the trailhead. You'll find that this is an excellent walk for a family with kids. Not only will they enjoy tramping over the boardwalks, but they will find birds, trees, and everything else carefully identified in the booklet for each turn of the trail. They can point out some eight different kinds of oak trees, spot wading birds, berries, mosses, numerous types of trees, and even learn to identify various birdcalls. If you want to introduce children to woodland walking amid wildflowers and great trees, you can't find a better trail.

The trail is open year-round, but is sometimes very wet. Be warned: stout shoes are a must because of wet footing, and the mosquito season is not a good time for a walk. Our choice is for an autumn hike. For information call the New Jersey Conservation Foundation at 908-234-1225.

🐝 The **Pemberton Rail Trail** is one of those special walks that makes you want to thank the hard-working citizens of a small town whose energies managed to save it. The 1.75-mile walk takes you from the North Pemberton Station (which is now a charming little museum of rail travel and natural wonders of the region) around and about some woods, two little rivers (the North Branch of the Rancocas and Budd's Run) and back to town again at the Birmingham Station.

The walk is on the just-wide-enough rail bed of a now defunct line of the Pennsylvania Railroad. The station, built in 1892 (replacing an earlier structure destroyed by fire), looks just like a rural station should. There are a couple of old cabooses on a siding, several donated old troop carrying cars of the type used at nearby Fort Dix in World War II, and here and there are some benches. Occasional structures, such as a bunkhouse for railroad workers, and tool sheds complete the nice picture. Railroad buffs will like the still-evident semaphores and other signals along the route. The going is flat and easy, and always picturesque. It is ideal for strollers and wheel chairs.

Open year-round, this trail is part of the Rails to Trails Conservancy. We recommend picking up the guide to the trail at the little museum shop. The museum is open Wednesday, Friday, Saturday, and Sunday from 10 A.M. to 4 P.M. Telephone: 609-894-0546.

Not far from Pemberton is another recommended site, with both historical and visual interest. The **Smithville County Park** is in an unusual spot. It is adjacent to a grand historic 1840 Greek Revival mansion and a factory and workers' homes that were the bailiwick of one Hezekiah Bradley Smith, who invented and manufactured such things as steam-run bicycles. The complex is next to a pretty little waterway (which once supplied his factory's power), and a lovely park and ravine. The creek runs in and out of the property—now the park—with steep banks and some spectacular vistas. You can walk down to the water at several different spots. And when you get to the bottom of the ravine walk—via some nice old stairs—you'll look out upon the greatest number of waterfowl we have ever seen. An extraordinary sight, and noisy too!

The first entrance (if you are driving from the south) is where the actual ravine walk begins. Make a left after the church, park along the road at the first or second small pull-off, and head into the woods. Following several different sandy paths (remember, you are near the Pine Barrens), you'll see the water down below. Follow the Ravine Nature Trail down some steep steps and there you are in a very special spot!

The second and third entrances are very picturesque, for here a dam and various old buildings will give you an idea of the layout of this unusual spot, obviously once a bustling enterprise and now almost completely deserted. You can walk either to a high site overlooking the creek (via the company houses on a small road) or through the parking lot to the water's edge, where trees lean over the creek and thousands upon thousands of black birds sit in the branches above you.

Walking areas are open year-round. The Smithville Mansion and the

Park Office are open for visitors and information. Telephone for hours: 609-261-3780.

 If you have kids in tow between September and Halloween, consider a walk through an extraordinary site: a seven-acre corn maze. **Bauma's Farm** turns its cornfields into a sight to behold each year. The great, high, cream-colored stalks that remain after the corn season are cut into various complex geometric designs. Kids will love a visit here. In fact, we recommend it for adults as well, for the experience is certainly different, particularly if you don't know exactly where you're going!

There is a charge for adults; kids under three are free. Telephone: 609-265-0888.

IN THE VICINITY
Sculpture Garden of Burlington County Community College
The Sculpture Garden of Burlington County Community College is in Pemberton on Route 530. The campus, which is quite pretty to walk around, maintains an unusual sculpture park, with a nice blend of contemporary sculpture and nature. You'll find a short walk there visually interesting, both for the art and the design of the garden. Telephone: 609-894-9311.

32 ·
WHARTON
STATE FOREST

Trails
and Vistas
in the
Pine Barrens

"Orange Trail," Mullica River in Wharton State Forest.

❧ HOW TO GET THERE

Batsto Village and Batsto Lake (Wharton State Forest)

From the Garden State Parkway, take exit 50 heading to New Gretna (Route 542). Continue west for 12.5 miles to park entrance.

Batona Trail, Yellow-Orange Trail

Walk through Batsto Village and turn right to find yellow/orange blazes at entrance.

Apple Pie Hill Fire Tower (Batona Trail)

From Batsto Village, take Route 542 (left turn out of park) to intersection with Route 563 toward towns of Jenkins, Speedwell, and Chatsworth. At Chatsworth take 532 west to entrance 1.5 miles on your left. Take dirt road (which winds around for about two miles) to the tower and park there.

The trails in this beautiful, unspoiled region are described as "sugar-sand." And that is a realistic description. Wide paths of pinkish white sand with a delicate carpet of pine needles make walking here soft and pleasurable. Around you are the famous scrub pines of the Pine Barrens, as well as wildflowers, bayberries and blueberries, wild orchids, and numerous other forest delights, interspersed with inky water holes reflecting the sky. There is an aroma of wild berries (we are in cranberry and blueberry country here). Songbirds abound. Delicate white butterflies dip in and out of view. Even on a hot day the tranquility of this lovely region makes you happy you ventured here. You can also enjoy this area on horseback; there are some 500 miles of sand roads open for riding. Canoeing areas are also available. (Be sure to take a map and a compass if you decide to take the deep-woods trails, though there are usually blazes.)

Wharton State Forest is an immense area, the largest single tract of land in the state parks system. It covers more than 110,000 acres in three adjacent counties. The iron bog industry flourished here in the Revolutionary War and War of 1812, when munitions were made from the local bog iron. But the decline of both the iron and glass industries led to the abandonment of the towns in the area. By the late nineteenth century it was a uniquely empty region of forests, rivers, and swampy bogs. In fact, some 17 trillion gallons of crystal-pure water sit just below ground level in the Pine Barrens and form one of New Jersey's most important aquifers.

In 1876 Joseph Wharton, a Philadelphia industrialist and financier, began assembling large areas of this unusual terrain; he intended to dam its streams and produce clean water for the growing cities nearby, which were suffering through a typhoid epidemic. But Wharton never succeeded; the vast tract was purchased by the state in 1954 as a watershed and recreation region, and all subsequent attempts to develop it have been foiled. Today it is almost completely a forested natural habitat, though occasional campsites and recreational areas can be found here and there on the peripheries of this great expanse.

One of those abandoned villages has been left intact. For about a century (1766 to 1867) **Batsto Village** (which comes from a Swedish and Leni-Lenape word meaning "bathing place") was once a busy bog iron and glass-making center; at one time 1,000 people lived here. The Batsto Iron Works functioned at this site from its founding in 1766, making such products as munitions, artillery fittings, wagons, ships, and kettles. Later, glass works were opened too. When Joseph Wharton bought the area he added a sawmill (still visitable) and an underground silo. He also created the elaborate four-story, Italianate villa (which you can tour), and began the cultivation of cranberries. Today, the twenty-eight buildings that comprised the town are a delightful place to walk. (You can get a self-guiding map at the Visitor Center.) Particular to its charm is the simple village architecture; many of the buildings are open and you can watch a number of craftspersons at work—among them a potter, candlemaker, basket weaver, chair caner. (No, they are not in period costumes). Among the pleasures are a gristmill, a rushing waterfall and hydraulic ram to pump the water, a charming bridge, a stone horse barn, and kilns and blacksmiths. In fact, if you want a taste of nineteenth-century-village America that is neither hokey nor commercial, this is it. In addition to the buildings, dotted throughout a flat area, you'll find the wide lawns and town greens, century-old trees, and wide, sandy pathways that make walking here a peaceful delight.

Batsto Village is open from 9 A.M. to 4:30 P.M. daily, year-round, except on major holidays. Guided tours are available. Fee only in summer season for admission and mansion tour. Telephone: 609-561-3262.

🐾 Off to the right as you walk through the village you'll come upon **Batsto Lake** (follow signs toward the Sawmill Nature Center). Created by a dam in 1766, this is the man-made lake that provided the waterpower for the iron and sawmill industries. It is a good-sized body of water with the first of our recommended trails around one side of it. A lovely sandy path (yellow blazes) runs alongside the lake amid sassafras, red oaks, cedars, and pitch pines, and in May and June pink lady-slippers and wild orchids. You'll delight in the aroma and the sight of waterfowl as well. Here and there you'll feel a soggy, springy sensation under your feet; this is an area of sphagnum moss, the bogs for which the area is known. After you've gone a little over a mile, the path veers away from the water and you'll find yourself on a quite soft sand trail through the woods and back to the village. The entire hike is a little more than two miles, but there are alternatives along the Lake: the red (blaze) trail is only seven-tenths of a mile, and the White trail is 3.8 miles.

Several additional trails begin near Batsto Village as well. Marked with colored blazes, each is shown on your self-guiding map, including the length of each walk. Our favorite is the Yellow/Orange Trail, accessed through a gate to your right, after you've walked through a good part of the village. This trail has several bridges over the Branch River's streams and ponds and is unusually lovely. Occasionally the pine and oak branches arch overhead, giving a true forest feeling, and then suddenly you are in the open again. A delightful bed of pine needles covers the sugar-sand pathway, the fragrance of wildflowers and berries is pervasive, and the dark, black, reflective inlets of the Branch River add both a cooling touch and contrasting colors to the scene. The lily pads and wild orchids and other wonderful growing things, interspersed with nice old-fashioned wooden bridges, make this a particularly pretty outing. You can also try the lovely, newly developed Tom's Pond Trail, which crosses and recrosses the Branch River several times.

The trails are open from dawn to dusk, year-round but can be crowded in summertime, when there is also a parking fee. Telephone: 609-561-3262.

The **Batona Trail** is the longest and most remote of the major trails within Wharton State Forest. It is ideal for true hikers, for it covers approximately 50 miles, starting in Lebanon State Forest and continuing both through Wharton and Bass River State Forests. (Of course, you can drive to various spots on the trail if you're not up to hiking 50 miles!) One part of the Batona Trail is accessible just beyond the main path of Batsto Village (ask for directions at the Visitor Center) and another entrance is at the Harrisville Lake on Route 679. The Batona Trail winds through the heart of the Pine Barrens and affords the most authentic, deep-woods experience of this unusual and vast pine and oak wilderness.

For an eight-mile round-trip outing on the Batona Trail, one of the best spots to start is at the **Apple Pie Hill Fire Tower** at the north end of Wharton State Forest. But first, try a vertical climb for one of the great views of the entire state. The Fire Tower, reached by car up a long, gradually climbing hill, is an old-fashioned construction that you are free to climb, step by step, for a vista of several states, the Atlantic Ocean, and the entire Pine Barrens. This is truly a magnificent sight!

The walk begins at the tower and continues (via pink blazes) into the wooded area, through golden heather, lichen, and blueberries (if you go in June) and pitch pines, cedar, and blackjack oak. Your path is soft and sandy, bordered here and there by lovely green moss. You'll relish the inky waterways (dark colored because of the tannin from tree leaves and bark that seep into the water) and the wooden bridges above and water lilies below. (If you are a birder or a wildflower enthusiast, pick up a list of what to listen and look for at the Visitor Center at Batsto Village before starting out; there are wonderful specimens—too numerous to note here—to be seen in the sandy expanses of the Pine Barrens.) If you walk the entire eight miles, you'll find an oddity: an obelisk dedicated to Emilio Carranza, "Mexico's Lone Eagle," a 23-year-old pilot who perished there in a thunderstorm on a solo flight in 1928. If four miles is more your distance, you can be picked up at the Carranza Monument instead of returning to the tower. Pick-up cars should take Carranza Road from Route 206, giving you about two and-a-half-hours to complete the four miles.

The Batona Trail is open daily, year-round. Take a compass and map with you, and follow blazes carefully. Parking at either the tower or Carranza Monument is free. Telephone: 609-561-3262.

IN THE VICINITY
Bass River State Forest

An Atlantic white cedar forest restoration project has been undertaken by environmentalists here (and in the future in Lebanon and Wharton State Forests, as well). Atlantic white cedar is a soft wood, and such forests were rapidly disappearing. This forest is a rather remote but beautiful place to walk; among its most enchanting sights is Lake Absegami, which is set in a 28-acre Natural Area of pinelands and trails (including a self-guided interpretive trail).

33·
CENTRAL JERSEY COAST

Birding at Edwin B. Forsythe National Wildlife Refuge.

Hidden Bikeways along the Shore: Birds and Marshes in Brigantine

🔥 HOW TO GET THERE

The Edwin B. Forsythe National Wildlife Refuge
(Brigantine division, at Oceanville)

Take the Garden State Parkway to exit 48; go south on Route 9 for six miles. Turn left onto Great Creek Road. Follow signs to refuge headquarters.

Great Bay Boulevard Wildlife Management Area

From Route 72, exit onto Route 9 and go south until you reach the town of Tuckerton. From the middle of town, turn left onto Great Bay Boulevard and follow until the end. Along the way you will cross five bridges (some quite narrow).

Manahawkin Wildlife Natural Area

Take Route 72 and exit onto Route 9; go north a short distance to Stafford Avenue (a right turn off Route 9) and continue straight into the preserve.

"The Shore" means different things to different people. While some think of pristine beaches, quiet waterside communities, and preserved natural areas, for others strip malls, lively gambling casinos, and miles of congested traffic come to mind. In fact, the shore includes both worlds, sometimes in close proximity.

In the peaceful preserves we describe below you are never too far from bustling areas—in some places you can even see Atlantic City's gambling casino towers in the background. But this fact in no way diminishes the great appeal of these natural wonders, and you appreciate them even more as precious oases.

The area we include in this outing—from the Brigantine region around Oceanville to the Barnegat region up north—is all part of the sprawling Edwin B. Forsythe National Wildlife Refuge, which extends along many coastal miles. The terrain is generally quite flat, making it ideal for biking—a recommended way to view nature. (Of course, you'll need to drive from one site to the next, given the distances.) So, pack up your bike and your binoculars and head off to this part of the shore for an unforgettable nature safari.

🦆 **The Edwin B. Forsythe National Wildlife Refuge** in the southernmost Brigantine region is a vast 40,000-acre birders' paradise with tidal marshes, open bays, channels, salt and freshwater meadows, sand islands, and woodlands. Situated in one of the Atlantic flyway's busiest flight paths, it provides a protected habitat for the thousands of migratory birds that rest, feed, and breed here. Depending on the season and time of day, you can spot any number of the 300 (at last count) species that visit regularly—snow geese, egrets, loons, pelicans, herons, cormorants, quail, gulls, terns, sandpipers, vultures—the list goes on and on.

The refuge dates from 1984, when two already existing conservation sites—Brigantine and Barnegat—were combined to preserve the habitats and migratory routes of certain threatened species (the black duck, for one).

The southern (Brigantine) section, easily accessible from Route 9, is a prime area for birders—undoubtedly its main draw. Included are two nature trails (for walkers), as well as a spectacular eight-mile self-guiding wildlife drive, also open to bikers and walkers. Before embarking on your exploration, make sure to stop at the refuge headquarters (near the parking lot) to pick up maps and a very comprehensive bird list. Also bring your binoculars, protective clothing (the sun can be quite intense at times) and bug repellant (mosquitoes and greenhead flies are pretty nasty during the summer).

The walking trails, Akers Woodland Trail and Leeds Eco-Trail, are both easy and short. The first is a one-fourth-mile path into a forest of black oak, holly, red cedar, and Virginia creepers. You might even spot white-tailed deer and owls.

The surprisingly diverse Leeds Eco-Trail is a slightly longer (half-mile) loop through salt marsh and forested uplands. A nice stretch of boardwalk (the first 700 feet of which is wheelchair friendly) takes you along the scenic wetlands, where the abundant salt marsh cordgrass sustains water birds, fiddler crags, clams, mullets, and other species. Great egrets, snow geese, and black ducks are frequent visitors. When you abruptly enter the woodsy part of this trail you find yourself in dense foliage of pine, oak, cedar, and sassafras. Watch for bees (they love the nectar from sassafras flowers), rabbits, foxes, and weasels. Thrushes, robins, and mockingbirds also live here.

The not-to-be-missed scenic drive is an elevated loop through wetlands and uplands. Along the way are several featured stops, where you are encouraged to get out of your car or off your bike and observe specific aspects of the wildlife and its habitat. (A list of things to look for is given to you at the entrance.) You see vast salt marshes and bays and little coves, as well as large freshwater pools created by diking (among the refuge's many managed activities). We were taken with the picturesque little islands dotting the marshes, surrounded by tall reeds—with postcard views of Atlantic City in the background. In these watery habitats you can spot numerous species of waterfowl, wading birds, and shorebirds, all making their raucous honks and squawks (it can be quite noisy at times!). You'll certainly see snow geese (who apparently are overpopulating the area), sandpipers, plovers, and every type of duck you can imagine. The marsh leads to a wooded coastal area, where, if you're lucky, you might chance upon a bald eagle.

The Forsythe National Wildlife Refuge is open year-round, dawn to dusk. There is a 4 dollar fee per car. Bear in mind that, although the refuge is a wonderful place to visit at any time of the year, the great waterfowl migrations occur in March–April and again in October–November, when the spectacle of so many thousands of birds all at once can be quite thrilling. Telephone: 609-652-1665.

A few miles away to the north is the **Great Bay Boulevard Wildlife Management Area**, another spectacular nature preserve ideal for both birding and biking. Here are more than 4,000 acres of pristine salt marshes graced with tall grasses and expansive water views.

This is truly an off-the-beaten-track place (much more so than Forsythe), reached by crossing a succession of narrow bridges (five of them) over a spit of land surrounded by Great Bay on one side and Little Egg Harbor on the other. If you are planning to bike there (about five miles), leave your car in the center of Tuckerton and head for Great Bay Boulevard; you'll ride past tall grasses, bays, and estuaries, and probably see only an occasional fisherman. At the end you can walk along a beach with shells and shorebirds and beautiful vistas over the sparkling water.

The site is always open and there is neither a fee nor a phone number to call. Just go and enjoy this rare, totally unspoiled, spot!

The **Manahawkin Wildlife Natural Area** is the northern-most section of the Forsythe Wildlife Refuge. If your taste runs to the remote, this is a place for you. For here, in the almost 1,000 acres of forest and marshland, is an area that will remind you of what our land must have looked like before large-scale settlement.

A wide, bumpy two- or three-mile dirt road carries you deep into the forest. Here are trees and undergrowth so thick that you cannot see into the depths of the woods. We saw only two obvious paths into this wilderness, where you might spot deer, quail, and woodcocks.

After a mile or two you'll come to a wonderful bog area. Water laps on either side of the road. You may leave your car or bike here (where it is unlikely anyone will pass it for hours or even days!) and walk along the bright yellow sand road between vast stretches of green sand marsh reeds. Cedar Creek runs alongside. Way in the distance is the arch of the bridge to Long Beach Island.

This is a choice spot for birding. Birds are everywhere: both water birds (ducks, mallards, teal) and forest birds swoop and swim, undisturbed. This is also a spot for crabbing. In fact, there is so much wildlife here that warnings are issued in hunting season. Be careful!

Manahawkin Natural Wildlife Area is always open. There are no amenities, no Visitor Center, and no entrance fees.

 **IN THE VICINITY**

Holgate (Edwin B. Forsythe National Wildlife Refuge), at the southern tip of Long Beach Island

If, after visiting Manahawkin, you're game for one more shore wildlife refuge before heading home, continue east on Route 72 onto Long Beach Island, turn right (south) onto Bay Avenue (Long Beach Boulevard), and go about nine miles to the parking area at the end. (As the crow flies, Holgate is just across the harbor from the Great Bay Boulevard Wildlife Management Area.)

In this pristine stretch of sandy beach are low dunes, mudflats, salt marshes, and, again, many, many birds. In fact, because Holgate is a federal refuge for endangered birds, people are not allowed to come during nesting season, from April 1 to August 30. Among the birds you might spot are egrets, plovers, terns, skimmers, sandpipers, and migrating barn swallows that stop along these shores in early September.

If you're looking for a quiet, contemplative experience and don't mind walking in soft sand (there is no other path), this 5.5-mile out-and-back island beachside walk is perfect. Besides watching the endlessly fascinating comings and goings of birds as they swoop down in search of their next meal, you can enjoy the mesmerizing waves washing ashore, the golden sunlight bathing the yellow sand, and the sea treasures that collect on the beach—driftwood, pebbles, shells.

Holgate is open from dawn to dusk daily, from September 1 to March 31. (Closed during nesting season.) There is no entrance fee. Telephone: 609-652-1665.

34·
ATLANTIC
COUNTY

*Short Walks
near
Atlantic City:
A Lakeside
Loop,
Exploring
a Coastal
Island, and
400,000
Orchids*

Path to the shore, Avalon.

HOW TO GET THERE

Heritage Park, Absecon

From the Garden State Parkway, take exit 40 to Route 30 heading south toward Absecon. Turn left (east) on Mill Road in Absecon, go two blocks and you'll see the park next to the municipal complex.

Brigantine Island

From Route 30 as above, take Route 87 to Brigantine Island and continue to Lighthouse Circle. Take Ocean Avenue to its end.

Waldor Orchids, Linwood

From the Garden State Parkway, take exit 36 to Tilton Road. At the first traffic light (Fire Road) turn right. Take Fire Road for 3.1 miles to Poplar Avenue. Make a left on Poplar; the greenhouses of Waldor Orchids are at 10 East Poplar Avenue.

Though this region is, of course, dominated by the high-rise hotels and gambling resorts of Atlantic City, there are several getaways worth noting. You'll enjoy these short walks, all within a few minutes of the metropolis; each is unusually lovely at any time of year.

Heritage Park in Absecon is a surprisingly bucolic public park. It has a very pretty 15-acre lake that is surrounded by a grassy knoll and walkways both at water level and above. You'll find yourself walking the eight-tenths of a mile in company with parading ducks and geese, a darling sight for small children. There are also canvasbacks, ospreys, and other birds (and many fish) cavorting in the waters. (Yes, the lake is stocked and fishing is allowed.) This secluded spot offers picnic tables and is altogether a very inviting spot for a short walk.

Brigantine Island will surprise you. (This outing is not in the remote northern section of the island that is part of the Edwin B. Forsythe National Wildlife Refuge.) Despite the densely packed houses and busy waterways of this resort community, there are two great walks to enjoy: an amazing beach walk, and a dune grass walk. If you follow the jam-packed roadway from Atlantic City through the island's residential areas, you'll come upon one of the widest, whitest, most inviting ocean beaches you can imagine. There is a boardwalk (actually a cement walk) bordering the end of the road (where you can leave your car) and a vast panorama to explore.

This delicious beach, where Captain Kidd is presumed to have buried his treasures, has some of the best air we have encountered on our many outings. The light, salty breezes you feel here are very special and will rejuvenate even the most tired family members. If you walk north on the beach you'll enjoy finding flotsam and jetsam brought in by the tide, as well as old pilings, roaring surf, and seashells. Eventually you'll come to Brigantine Inlet, an area of dangerous shoals (and many shipwrecks) and spectacular views. This walk is about two miles each way.

If you prefer walking on a hard-packed trail just behind the beach, the island offers that option too. Just beyond the boardwalk's northern end, turn left and walk into the dune grass behind the beach. Here you can pick up a very lovely trail that parallels the beach and is surrounded with bayberry, grasses, beach plums, and other plants natural to the Atlantic coastline. Birds love this area. You will have the same ocean breezes but a different type of experience, for the foliage rises high around you so there is a great sense of privacy about this walk. We saw not one other hiker on our outing.

A little farther south, at Avalon, is Seven Mile Beach, considered one of the best dune-and-beach sites on the coast. (The World Wildlife Fund owns a vast stretch of wetlands here too.) You'll walk on the finest sand to be found on the Jersey shore. Telephone: 609-652-1665.

Waldor Orchids is an entirely different experience, but we think it's a great treat. This indoor walk takes you from greenhouse to greenhouse in an amazing complex of indoor gardens—all of them featuring orchids. This enterprise began in 1927, and now Walter and George Off and a dozen members of their family are continuing a long tradition of growing orchids. Some 400,000 orchids grow here. You will see every color and size imaginable, some shipped from Hawaii to mature here in New Jersey, others cultivated right here.

The beauty of these delicate blooms is exquisite, and the people are very friendly, allowing the visitor to roam about and enjoy the sights and fragrances. Some of the areas are showplaces, much like indoor botanical garden settings, with small waterfalls, rocky outcroppings, and everywhere orchids. We recommend this walk to any garden lovers.

Waldor Orchids is open to the public two days per week, or by appointment. Telephone: 609-927-4126.

35·
CAPE MAY
COUNTY

Wetlands Institute marshland.

New Jersey's Southern Coastline:
A Boardwalk, a Seawall, and
Sandy Paths through Remote Marshes
and along Coastal Inlets

 HOW TO GET THERE

Corson's Inlet State Park

From the Garden State Parkway, take exit 25. Follow Roosevelt Avenue east and turn south on Scenic Drive in Ocean City. Continue south until it becomes a highway surrounded by marshlands and follow signs; entrance to the park is on your right.

The Wetlands Institute, Stone Harbor

From the Garden State Parkway, take exit 10. Go east on Stone Harbor Boulevard for three miles. The Institute is at number 1075, on your right just before the Stone Harbor Bridge.

Hereford Inlet, Anglesea (North Wildwood)

From the Garden State Parkway, take exit 6 (North Wildwood). At exit ramp turn right onto Route 147. It will become New Jersey Avenue. Make a left at Chestnut, and go two blocks to Central Avenue. The parking lot for the Hereford Inlet Lighthouse is at 111 North Central Avenue. (There is another parking area at the other end of the seawall, farther east.)

You may think of Cape May as a popular resort, filled with lovely Victorian homes and great beaches. But Cape May County also has a wonderful and surprising coastline that is available to walkers who enjoy remote and beautiful coastal scenery (and bird watching, too.) We found these three sites particularly appealing, for they were virtually empty of visitors, and the ambience of the coast—the sights and smells and tangy air—is delightful.

Corson's Inlet State Park with its coastal wetlands is hidden away just beyond the hustle and bustle of Ocean City. The inlet is a very picturesque waterway where people who enjoy boating can put their craft into the sea. For those of us who want to hike, this is an unusual spot indeed. (There is no park information or headquarters.) This is a large semicircle of an inlet divided at one side by a bridge. Just below the Corson's Inlet Bridge, you'll find a small parking area where you can leave your car. You'll see an occasional fisherman or birdwatcher here, but basically you will have an inviting expanse of beach, dune grass, and a fine network of paths to explore quite alone here.

Sandy trails just near the beach will take you through some small coastal dunes, with silver driftwood, bayberries, and other delightfully beachy plants edging the soft paths. This is one walk you can do barefoot. Most of the trails end up again on the shore, so it is hard to get lost. Needless to say, birds abound here (as does poison ivy in some parts). You can also hike along the inlet's beach itself. This rarely visited shore is great for beach combing, particularly if you like collecting shells and driftwood.

For information call the Belleplain State Forest at 609-861-2404.

The Wetlands Institute provides a very different experience. The state of New Jersey has done an exemplary job since 1970 of saving its wetlands. We were astonished to discover that the state has almost 250,000 acres of salt marsh—now, of course, recognized as essential to our ecosystem. Among the many endangered species of wildlife that breed and live in these 6,000 acres of wetlands are the bog turtle, ospreys, and the great blue heron.

The Institute is a nonprofit center where you can find out why we save our wetlands, both in museum exhibits ("Secrets of the Salt Marsh"), and by walking on a boardwalk through these wonderful marshes. There is also an observation tower, a children's discovery room, and an aquarium, with such delights as seahorses.

The trail itself is both evocative and educational. The slightly elevated boardwalk that moseys through these inimitable marshes even allows you to step down here and there into the squishy surface of the marsh to examine flora and fauna. (For example, you might spot little holes in the wet surface—the burrows of fiddler crabs.) The air is fresh and salty. You'll find this is a prime birding spot, featuring birds migrating in fall and spring and nesting in summer; there are waterfowl year-round. (If you are a serious bird watcher, you might also want to get directions at the office for the Stone Harbor Bird Sanctuary nearby.)

Thirteen stops are marked on this trail, each with a small information plaque. We loved our walk along this very flat boardwalk, our vistas completely empty of civilization, the tall reed grasses and delicate shrubs, beach plum bushes, and marsh elder waving gently in the breeze. Here and there we came upon little screen-covered dishes with Do Not Touch signs. These turned out to be nesting spots for the endangered turtles.

This is definitely a recommended place for taking the children. Not only is there lots to interest them at the Institute (where they can hold various sea creatures in their hands), but the walk itself is undemanding, with benches for resting all along its length.

A trail guide is available at the headquarters. Visits here are recommended any time of the year, and there are a number of special events, all relating to the salt marsh. The Institute is open daily from 9:30 A.M. to 4:30

P.M., closed Sunday and Monday from October 15 to May 15. Telephone: 609-368-1211.

🐝 If you love strolling along the oceanside but find walking in the sand is not your favorite pastime, try the seawall walk at **Hereford Inlet**. This is a most unusual spot, combining a great vista of the sea, a secure and solid footing for your walk, a charming garden at the end, and a visit to a pretty little lighthouse.

The lighthouse here, a historic and charming building that you can climb up, sits on the south side of the coastal inlet. The Victorian-style lighthouse, which dates to 1874, guarded generations of sailors from the shifting sandbars and shoals of this seaside spot. Anglesea was a fishing village, right at the edge of the Inland Waterway, which runs from Maine to Florida, and the lighthouse at Anglesea has had a long and illustrious history. (A flier detailing its story is available at the small shop there.) We recommend a climb to the top, particularly if you have children with you.

Adjacent to the lighthouse is a very pretty, award winning English-cottage garden. After your walk along the seawall, you will enjoy resting here amid the profusion of flowers and shrubbery, birdbaths and borders, all planted according to an unusually charming plan. This is a garden for garden enthusiasts. It has 170 varieties of plantings, carefully arranged and, like so many seaside gardens, is gloriously profuse.

Take the few steps up to the seawall from the garden. You will find the very opposite of the carefully arranged plantings along this wide rocky breakwater. Here wild beach grasses and other natural vegetation lines one side as you make your way above the beach and sea. This is a nice walk that continues for quite a distance, with the town to one side and the ocean on the other. You might see such coastal birds as pelicans, ospreys, cormorants, and herring gulls on this walk. (Though it does not have a completely smooth surface, wheeled vehicles such as strollers and wheelchairs can be pushed along this seawall top, which has been evened out with cement. There is also a place for picking up walkers at the other end so you do not have to retrace your steps.)

For information, call the Hereford Inlet Lighthouse at 609-522-4520. The lighthouse is open daily in summertime, from 9 A.M. to 7 P.M.; in spring and fall through Christmas, from 11 A.M. to 4 P.M.

36·
CAPE MAY

Cape May, waterfowl.

New Jersey's Southern Tip: Birds, Butterflies, Breakwater, and Beaches

🌿 HOW TO GET THERE

Cape May Point State Park

Take the Garden State Parkway to its end (just north of Cape May) and follow signs for the center of town. Make a right at the "T" onto Sunset Boulevard (Route 606); after about two miles turn left onto Lighthouse Avenue and go less than a mile to the park entrance, on your left.

Cape May Migratory Bird Refuge

The refuge is very near Cape May Point State Park, off Sunset Boulevard (Route 606), on the ocean side.

Cape May Bird Observatory

The observatory is located on East Lake Drive, off Lighthouse Avenue.

Higbee Beach Wildlife Management Area

From Route 607 (Bayshore Road), turn left onto Route 641 (New England Road) to its end; park and follow a little dirt road leading to the beach.

It's easy to see why Cape May is a popular tourist destination. The town itself draws visitors for its charming turn-of-the-century houses, cozy inns, and eclectic boutiques. But Cape May offers many natural wonders, too. Surrounding it are inviting woodlands and some of the prettiest beaches on the Atlantic coast, ideal for walking, fishing, and swimming.

Cape May is also a birder's paradise. In fact, it is considered to be one of the best birding spots in North America. On this southernmost tip of New Jersey, tens of thousands of migrating birds congregate on their long journeys between the Arctic tundra and South America, and refuel on the ever-abundant horseshoe crabs. Sometimes birds flying south must wait patiently for favorable winds before making the 13-mile crossing over Delaware Bay; then they become backed up (much like planes on an airstrip), adding to their already prodigious numbers.

Like birds, butterflies are also profuse in the Cape May region, for basically the same reasons. The diverse habitats including salt and freshwater wetlands, natural grasslands, and oak and pine woodlands attract more than 100 butterfly species. Each fall there is a famous Monarch butterfly migration through the Cape, one which brings lepidopterists and butterfly fanciers to the region.

Following are some of the best natural sites to explore within Cape May, whether you come to spot birds or butterflies, to enjoy a walk along a scenic beach, or simply to take in ocean breezes. Note that Cape May is most appealing off season, after the summer crowds have gone. Fall is undoubtedly the best time to observe migrating birds and butterflies, although walking on the beach and nearby woodland trails is a treat in winter and spring, too.

🦋 **Cape May Point State Park** offers among the most scenic ocean vistas we have found anywhere in the state. Situated right on the southwest tip of Cape May, where the Atlantic Ocean and Delaware Bay meet, the 190-acre park includes beautiful beachfront dunes and a natural wooded area with walking trails along freshwater marshes and little ponds. Facing the ocean is a 157-foot tall historic lighthouse dating from 1859 but still in use today. (For a small fee you can climb to the top for an amazing panoramic view.)

The land where the park is now located was used by the navy as a strategic defense site during World War II. In fact, one of the several bunkers that were built along the shore still stands (the others were lost to beach erosion and storms). The park was officially established in 1974 and military buildings were transformed into the Visitor Center and the Environmental Education Center. We recommend you stop at the Visitor Center to pick up maps, brochures, and information on birds and butterflies, hawk watches, and other activities before starting off.

Most of the park (153 acres) has been designated as the Cape May Point Natural Area, home to ducks, herons, seagulls, and swans. It's also a critical nesting and feeding area for thousands of migrating birds (including some 17 different species of hawks) and monarch butterflies. Three miles of walking trails crisscross beach habitats, wetlands, and woods where some of these species can be spotted. Several raised platforms are scattered about, including one overlooking the freshwater marsh, ideal for viewing hawks.

The trail head is at the edge of the large parking area and leads to a lovely boardwalk surrounded by very tall marsh reeds, or phragmites. You can choose from three well-marked and color-coded trails, including a half-mile loop (the red trail) specifically designed for wheelchairs. Another, the two-mile blue trail, meanders through red cedar woodlands, marshes, and swamps, over little bridges and past observation platforms, eventually reaching high dunes overlooking the ocean (please note that you must stay off the dunes); the trail then circles back along the beach toward the light-house, passing the remaining bunker along the way. The walking is easy and quite flat.

The park is open daily, dawn to dusk, year-round. The Visitor Center is open daily (summer hours are 8 A.M. to 8 P.M.; check off-season hours). Telephone: 609-884-2159.

🐛 If you're feeling energetic, you can reach our second site, the **Cape May Bird Migratory Refuge**, from Cape May Point State Park on foot by heading east along the beach for about one mile. If you prefer going by car, drive back to Sunset Boulevard and look for signs to the refuge. Known as "The Meadows," the refuge is a lovely, rustic place for bird (and butterfly) watching. Maintained by the Nature Conservancy, it includes several blinds for observing the hundreds of species that appear along the shore-line during various times of the year.

Leave your car at the parking area just off the road and walk along the little path just beyond, which leads to the ocean through marshlands in a short time. You will find yourself surrounded by tall grasses, reeds, and bayberry bushes, with spectacular water views on either side. The walking is flat and easy, with boardwalk, grass, and deliciously soft sand underfoot.

This is a peaceful spot, where you will only hear the sounds of birds and ocean waves lapping along the shore. Most visitors are serious birders with binoculars in hand, hoping no doubt to catch sight of the more exotic species. A comprehensive checklist of birds and butterflies found in Cape May County is available at Cape May Point State Park or Cape May Bird Observatory.

Once on the beach, you can walk in either direction for miles. To your right (facing the ocean) you'll see Cape May Point State Park with its unmistakable lighthouse in the distance.

The refuge is open at all times of the year, from sunrise to sunset.

🐛 Cape May has a few additional spots primarily for butterflies. One is the nearby **Cape May Bird Observatory** where, if you are so inclined, you might stop to see its tiny (only one-fourth acre) but pretty butterfly gar-den. Here, amid bee balm, bleeding heart, and other plantings that seem to attract these enchanting little creatures, you can find monarchs, mourning cloaks, and many other kinds of butterflies—as well as hummingbirds, which apparently like the same plants.

The observatory also has a comprehensive information center that offers workshops on birds and butterflies, as well as books and brochures on these subjects. It also conducts a popular annual hawk watch, when viewers might see up to 1,000 hawks at a time.

The butterfly garden is open daily, year-round, dawn to dusk. There is no charge. The observatory is open daily, from 10 A.M. to 5 P.M. Telephone: 609-884-2736.

Higbee Beach Wildlife Management Area includes 886 acres of holly and oak woodlands, fields, ponds, a jetty, high dunes covered with beachgrass and honeysuckle, and more than a mile of spectacular beach with great views. The diverse habitats attract songbirds (in addition to hawks, bald eagles, and falcons), migrating in huge numbers, from late August to October.

The beach itself is a lovely, wide expanse of white sand along Delaware Bay. At the end is a long breakwater that stretches into the town harbor; children (and spirited adults, too) won't be able to resist climbing on the big rocks that form the jetty. From the beach you can often see ferry boats passing by on their way to and from Lewes, Delaware, across the wide bay.

This is a great spot for children. There are treasures to be found in the soft white sand. Look for driftwood, shells (especially those left by horseshoe crabs), beach plums (great for making preserves), and the so-called Cape May diamonds. These "gems" are actually shiny quartz pebbles; they used to be more plentiful, prompting Higbee Beach to be known also as Diamond Beach, a name that remains.

Besides strolling on the beach, you have a choice of several (unfortunately not well marked) trails that start at the parking area, leading into the woods and circling back onto the beach. Find the information board at the parking area for more details. Note, too, that fishing, horseback riding, and hunting are allowed, with permits, in some sections of the park. (Hunting begins in early November, after bird migration season.)

Higbee Beach Wildlife Management Area is open year-round, from dawn to dusk. There is no entrance fee. Telephone: 609-292-2965.

37·
DELAWARE BAY REGION

Biking the Remote South Jersey Coast: An Island, Salt Marshland, Sandy Beaches, and a Historic Lighthouse

Delaware Bay's East Point Lighthouse.

⚓ HOW TO GET THERE

Moores Beach

From the Garden State Parkway, take exit 17 to Route 9 south. Turn west on Route 83 and continue to its intersection with Route 47 (north). Just past the small town of Delmont, turn left on Moores Beach Road. (Park your car when the road becomes dirt; this is no place to drive.)

East Point Lighthouse

From Route 47 as above, take Glade Road left just past Moores Beach Road. Follow signs to Lighthouse Road.

Egg Island

Take Route 47 north as above, continuing on to Mauricetown (see below). Pick up Route 670 (also called Dividing Road) there and go south, following signs to Dividing Creek. There are two entrances to Egg Island from Maple Street in Dividing Creek: one follows Maple Street to its end over a causeway; the other goes to Turkey Point on Turkey Point Road.

Those travelers who think they know New Jersey well, being familiar with its busy corridors and sophisticated towns, will be astonished to find this region. This is as remote an area as any you will find in the most rural areas of our country. You will be hard pressed to come upon even a gas station where this outing takes you. And certainly no restaurants, nor any convenience stores dot the winding byways. But the Delaware Bay area of the state is a desolate and beautiful region that lends itself to biking; the spaces are wide, the roads are flat, and the air is filled with sea breezes off the vast bay.

Once home to a thriving oystering and seafaring industry, this natural marshland and beachfront region is now almost deserted. (One town we passed through listed seven residents.) The oysters were depleted many years ago by a parasite, putting as many as five hundred oyster sailing boats out of business. With bustling Cape May and the Atlantic Ocean coast within an hour's drive, there has apparently been little effort to turn this area into a resort, though there are lovely white sand beaches dotted with shells. There are expansive stretches of marshland that have some of the best bird watching in the entire state, but we saw few people actually using their binoculars to spot the soaring hawks and blue herons above our heads. There are one or two small historic towns, once home to sea captains (who built the imposing Victorian homes that still stand), but there are no commercial regions and the streets are eerily quiet. If getting away from it all into a remote and haunting landscape is your idea of fun, try these routes. (And bring your own lunch.)

Moores Beach faces south, like all of the beaches along this part of the coast. It has delicious white sand. But getting there is the hard part. When you leave your car at the end of the paved area, you will find an almost impossibly pitted dirt road that is nevertheless passable by bike or foot. It leads you through a desolate marshland toward the sea. Almost the only trees among the high reeds are gray stumps, though there are occasional clumps of pine and oak. There is water everywhere: inlets, little bays, meandering creeks. Hawks circle overhead. Moores Beach is part of the Heislerville Wildlife Management Area, more than 4,000 acres of salt-hay marsh, some of it diked, and all of it beautiful, in a quiet, reflective way. There are birds aplenty, particularly during fall and spring migrations (sandpipers, turnstones, red knots, and many other birds), and waterfowl all of the time. In May, horseshoe crabs spawn on the beach here. This is about a two-hour walk but of course is much faster by bike.

In this remote area **East Point Lighthouse** is a particularly inviting site; it is also surrounded by the same tidal marshes, whose reeds reach up well over one's head—perhaps to nine or ten feet. The second oldest lighthouse in New Jersey (after Sandy Hook), East Point was built in 1849. It is a very charming, whitewashed brick structure that provided oyster schooners with guidance; it is presently the only functioning light on Delaware Bay. A walk here (leave your bike at the lighthouse) will take you through the marshes right to the beach, where you can stroll for a short distance. You can hear the lapping waves from the lighthouse, as well as the inviting calls of gulls and other shore birds. During the summer months the lighthouse sponsors a variety of events, including a marsh walk.

Egg Island cannot be called the "highpoint" of such a flat and marshy region, but it is definitely the best place in this area for a get-away by bike. A large area (over 8,000 acres), it is reached by causeway, and is indeed an island. Not only is it surrounded by water, but it has inlets and streams galore. There is fishing for sea bass and fluke and bluefish here. Numerous white swans were swimming in one small cove when we went through. The long, windy roads—there are several of them—are made mostly of crushed shells, and their white surface gleams in the bright ocean air. On either side of you, high reeds wave in the wind. The easternmost road winds around the island quite indefinitely—there are no maps or signs, only an occasional old hay wagon leaning against the marsh. If you take the Turkey Point Road you'll find a clearer route with occasional signs; there is a well-built bird-viewing platform of the marshland below, and there are peregrine falcon nesting towers here.

IN THE VICINITY
Mauriceville and Greenwich
Mauriceville and Greenwich are two very small towns that boast fine Victorian houses, once built by sea captains, in unusual tidal-marsh settings. The Maurice River is a winding, picturesque river that carried oyster schooners inland from the bay; today it is very pretty, with an old (now unused) drawbridge and a tiny park with a vista of the river and the marshes. Greenwich, another charming village, is similarly situated near the Cohansey River at Delaware Bay.

38·
SOUTH-CENTRAL
NEW JERSEY

Village Green, Wheaton Village.

Treats in Three Rural Counties:
A Spectacular State Park, a Craft Village,
an Arboretum, and a Remote Forest

🔥 HOW TO GET THERE

Parvin State Park

Parvin State Park is in southern Salem County along the Cumberland County border. Park entrance is on Route 540, six miles west of Vineland and one mile east of Centerton. To get there from northern locations, take the New Jersey Turnpike south to exit 3; follow signs for I-295 west (you will be on it a very short distance), I-676 south to Route 55 south. Stay on Route 55 south to exit 45. Continue south on Route 553 for about eight miles to Centerton, then take Route 540 (going east) for about two miles. Follow park signs.

Wheaton Village, Millville

Millville, in Cumberland County, is halfway between Philadelphia and Atlantic City, a few miles southeast of Parvin State Park. From Route 55 (see above), take exit 26 and follow Wheaton Village signs (in brown) to the main entrance at 1501 Glasstown Road. Or, if you're going there directly from northern locations: Take the New Jersey Turnpike south to exit 4; take Route 73 north to I-295 south. Stay on I-295 south to Route 42 south, then take Route 55 south to exit 26. Turn right and then left onto Wade Boulevard. Entrance is one-half mile down on the right.

Scotland Run Park, Clayton

The park is located in Gloucester County (north of both Parvin State Park and Millville), a few miles south of Glassboro, just east of Route 47, at the intersection of Route 655 (Fries Mill Road) and Route 610 (Clayton-Williamstown Road).

Glassboro Wildlife Management Area

This site is located just northeast of Clayton, east of Route 47 and south of Route 322.

New Jersey continues to surprise and delight us with its variety of green spaces and points of interest, even in the more off-the-beaten-traditional-tourist-track parts of the state. Take, for instance, the south-central region, southeast of Philadelphia. In this somewhat sparsely populated area there are, nonetheless, places that are fun and interesting to explore on foot.

The three sites we describe below are relatively close to one another, though located within three separate counties: Salem, Cumberland, and Gloucester. Two are lovely parks (one more rustic, the other includes an arboretum), and the third is a craft village featuring glassworks.

🐾 **Parvin State Park**, easily one of the region's gems, is a small (when it comes to state parks) preserve of just over 1,000 acres. Hidden away in a remote section of southern Salem County, along the Cumberland County border, it contains an unusual variety of plant and animal life because it is located quite far south, in a transition zone between two ecosystems. Throughout the park are many kinds of trees, shrubs, ferns (we had no idea such a variety of ferns existed!), club mosses, and flowering plants. Among the more unusual are spectacular groves of holly trees, some even reaching 40 feet; with their bright red berries and shiny dark green leaves, they add a look of Christmas on snowy winter days. Migrant and nesting birds are everywhere (there are over 100 species), and you might encounter salamanders, turtles, toads, river otters, raccoons, deer, foxes, weasels, and muskrats lurking about in the dense foliage.

Parvin also has two lakes (Parvin and Thundergust), a stream (Muddy Run Creek), a winding gorge, and many nice—though not particularly well marked—hiking trails. (Fortunately, the park office sells excellent detailed maps, a must for any serious walker.) All the trails are open to bikers and horseback riders as well as walkers. In winter you might see cross-country skiers gliding along; in summer, campers come to enjoy these great outdoors (camping is available on the lake shores).

Among the park's most varied trails is a 4.6-mile loop starting at Parvin Lake and connecting with the Long Trail. (Check at the park office for its exact location.) You'll go along both lakes and the creek, and through a floodplain and cedar swamp. Along the way you'll come across a wonderful sampling of diverse plants, including those grand hollies, as well as magnolias, black tupelos, eastern burning bushes (spectacular bright orange visions in the fall). The lakes are rich with bird life, too: great blue herons are among the aquatic species that can often be spotted wading along the shores. (Bring along your binoculars and bird/nature guides.) This is a relatively easy walk, with few ups and downs, one that children can also enjoy.

Parvin was developed during the Depression, when the Civilian Conservation Corps created its network of trails, campgrounds, and wooden bridges; it became a state park soon after. During the war, the workers' barracks were actually used to house German prisoners of war and, later, interned Japanese Americans from the West Coast.

The park is open daily, year-round, dawn to dusk, free of charge. (The park office is open daily during the summer; off-season, from October to May, it is open only on week days.) Telephone: 856-358-8616.

🌼 While Parvin State Park is a quiet spot, **Wheaton Village** in Millville is anything but. This bustling crafts center includes a famous glass factory (where you can watch the fascinating transformation of hot molten glass into objects), a museum of glassworks (with 6,500 items on display), and rows of artists' studios and artsy shops.

There is a lot to see and do here, and more than 90,000 visitors (including families with children) come each year. The village is fun to explore, with its many galleries, shops, artifacts, museums, and historic buildings (the 1876 schoolhouse, for one). Craft demonstrations are frequently offered, from glassmaking (by far the most popular) to pottery, woodworking, and tinsmithing. But you need not be only an observer; you can participate actively in making objects, such as creating your own paperweight, should you so desire. (Paperweights are apparently popular items in Wheaton Village, with a shop claiming to contain the world's largest collection!)

The T. C. Wheaton Glass Factory is a must. Here you can watch artisans shaping, blowing, and molding the hot glass using nineteenth-century techniques to create household objects of all shapes and sizes. Annual events—including antique and car shows—and special exhibitions are also a part of the Wheaton Village experience. (Phone the central office for information on upcoming events.)

But there is nature here too, with great trees, a village green, and a lake, as you will see on your map. The town of Millville's importance dates to the late nineteenth century, when it was the center of New Jersey's glass industry. Its downtown is now being revitalized as a regional cultural center and is worth a detour. If you have time, stroll on the Riverwalk, which includes a pleasant boardwalk along the Maurice River.

Wheaton Village itself is open daily, April to December from 10 A.M. to 5 P.M., and during the winter months from Wednesday to Sunday. Entrance fees. Telephone: 800-998-4552 or 856-825-6800.

🌼 **Scotland Run Park,** near the town of Clayton in Gloucester County, is the largest of the county parks, with its 940 acres of greenery. Besides a lovely 80-acre lake (popular for boating, fishing, and swimming), there are walking trails, a beach, bog garden, self-guided trail, and a pretty arboretum featuring a good variety of trees. The Nature Center includes displays of the flora and fauna of the region, as well as information and trail maps.

❧ The park is very near the **Glassboro Wildlife Management Area**, a vast (2,337-acre) region preserved in a pristine state and used primarily by hunters and fishermen. Walkers will find Scotland Run a more "civilized" choice; its upland woods and vistas are similar, and it is a more accessible (and safer) option. But if you prefer your experiences of nature to be remote and even desolate, try this wildlife management area. It is definitely a "forest primeval."

Scotland Run Park and Glassboro Wildlife Management Area are both open daily all year, from dawn to dusk, free of charge. However, the Nature Center at Scotland Run is only open on weekdays from 9 A.M. to 3 P.M. Telephone: 856-881-0845 or 856-468-0100.

39·
DELAWARE RIVER REGION

Supawna Meadows National Wildlife Refuge.

The Mouth of the Delaware:
Historic Sites and Water Views

 HOW TO GET THERE

Red Bank Battlefield

From Route 295, take exit 23 at National Park. Go through the town to the western edge and banks of the Delaware River; the Battlefield is at 100 Hessian Avenue, National Park, N.J.

Fort Mott State Park

Take Route 295 south to intersection with Route 40, and continue south on Route 49. (Do not cross Delaware River.) When you have passed the town of Pennsville, look for Fort Mott Rd., which will take you to the park.

Supawna Meadows National Wildlife Refuge and Finn's Point Rear Range Light

This area is adjacent to Fort Mott. Follow directions above.

Battlefields and the surroundings of long-ago forts and lighthouses are some of our oldest preserved spaces. They used to be the only areas left untouched by development of any kind, and as such have frequently been visited by people who like open areas and places to walk—as well as a touch of history as they go. Red Bank Battlefield, Fort Mott, and Finn's Point Rear Range Light have distinctive historic qualities in great settings, surrounded by water and scenic vistas. And the nearby Supawna Meadows National Wildlife Refuge is as remote and beautiful a spot as you could ask for.

You'll find that **Red Bank Battlefield** is an entirely different type of green walk from most of the outings in this book. Battlefields are almost always interesting sites for walking, with or without the graphic descriptions that are often posted along the way. And, as some of the only unspoiled land in many areas, they offer grand open spaces that are usually lovingly maintained. (This is an odd phenomenon—seen in other countries, too—where the site of historic carnage and destruction becomes a major recreational area.)

Red Bank Battlefield is no exception. It is a very lovely green sward along the vast Delaware River. Its great expanse overlooking the water has groves of great trees, piers, pavilions, the remains of a fort, monuments, and a historic house. You couldn't ask for a nicer or more attractive picnic spot; it is breezy, nonwoodsy, and peaceful.

It wasn't always so peaceful. During the Revolutionary War the Americans won a battle here at Fort Mercer (the remains of this structure are still visible), successfully blockading the Delaware River with huge iron chains (on view). The wounded were tended at the 1748 Whitall House within the park (visitable). A 75-foot monument to this historic battle sits in the north end of the park.

There are two trails or courses for walking. (Pick up a map at the Ranger Office near the parking lot.) The mile-long route begins at the parking lot and crosses the vast lawn from one pavilion to the other and then takes you along the river to the northern end, where it loops back at the ruins of Fort Mercer. A shorter walk of one-half mile includes the riverside promenade, returning near the park's own roadway.

Red Bank Battlefield is open dawn to dusk. The house is open weekends from 1 P.M. to 4 P.M. throughout the summer, or by appointment. Telephone: 856-853-5120.

Fort Mott State Park is at one of the tip ends of New Jersey, near the mouth of the Delaware River. Its 104 acres surround an old fort (bring the kids!), and though there are no great historical moments in its past, it nonetheless is an interesting and inviting place for a walk (and for fishing and crabbing too).

Built in 1896–97, it was named for Gershom Mott, a Civil War major general and native of New Jersey. It functioned until after World War II, when it was decommissioned and its armaments were removed. Today it is a solitary spot, with a lot of open space, a few picnic grills, and lovely views.

The park is open daily from 8 A.M. to 8 P.M. from Memorial Day through Labor Day, and from 8 A.M. to 4 P.M. the rest of the year. Telephone: 856-935-3218.

Supawna Meadows National Wildlife Refuge is adjacent to Fort Mott, at the southeastern corner of the park. This wildlife refuge is huge, containing some 2,500 acres of woodlands and water access. The Salem River runs through it. There is limited hunting (we prefer not to visit in fall), and always excellent bird watching.

Of particular note is the lighthouse, called the **Finn's Point Rear Range Light**. In this remote spot a lighthouse is literally a beacon to the outside world. This one was built in 1876 and is on the National Record of Historic Places. You can actually visit the lighthouse on occasion, and get a different vista of this wild and somewhat desolate—but beautiful—spot from above.

The lighthouse is open on the third Sunday of each month from April through October, from noon to 4 P.M. Telephone: 856-935-1487.

40·
EAST OF
PHILADELPHIA

Palmyra Cove Nature Park.

*A Forest, a Native American
Reservation, a Freshwater Tidal
Marsh, and an Old Apple Orchard*

 HOW TO GET THERE

Rancocas Nature Preserve

From Route 295, take exit 45A, east on Rancocas Road. Go 1.8 miles; the entrance is on your right at 794 Rancocas Rd., Mount Holly.

Palmyra Cove Nature Park

From Route 295, take exit 36 to Route 73 north. Take Route 73 for about five miles and turn right on Souder Street, to second left. You'll see Bridge Commission Offices on your right. (Be careful not to cross Tacony Bridge!) Follow road around Bridge Commission building, down under bridge, where you'll see a small parking area on your right.

The Barclay Farmstead Gardens

Located in Cherry Hill, the farm is at 209 Barclay Lane. Take exit 4 of the New Jersey Turnpike to parallel I-295 south. Take exit 34 off Route 295, onto Route 70. You'll find Barclay Lane just off Route 70.

The woodsy and very pretty **Rancocas Nature Preserve** (and Audubon Center) has several surprises to offer the walker. We first must tell you that the most essential surprise is that it is filled with forking paths, has no blazes, and the map provided at the headquarters is woefully inadequate. Though the entire area is 1,100 acres and the parts with trails are much less than that, you can (and we did) get thoroughly lost. Breadcrumbs and a compass might help! But having warned you, we urge you not to hesitate to take this walk, for it offers several particularly nice aspects.

You'll begin at an old white barn, entering a shady wooded path and bearing left. Your first and most stunning surprise—and what sets this wooded walk apart from so many others—is the orderly pine forest you soon come upon. Planted on a farm field less than 50 years ago, (each tree was only about a foot tall then), these rows of Norway spruce, American white pine, and Austrian pine create one of the most remarkable forest scenes we've seen. Towering overhead, these long rows of tall, straight conifers provide only a glimpse of the sky. You'll be walking on the softest of surfaces: deep, deep pine needles (indeed, not much else cares to grow in this environment), where the army of pines in elegant formation dominates both land and sky. Give yourself time to enjoy this sight.

Continue on the path, which has occasional numbered informational signs corresponding to the self-guiding map. You will soon come to Rancocas Creek, bordered by holly and oak. This is thoroughly picturesque; it makes you think of primeval America as it winds through the woods, trees, and vines, and the wildflowers dipping into its dark waters.

And, in fact, bearing left, you can take a detour here and find yourself adjacent to one of the state's only Native American reservations. (See below for a proper visit.) The nature preserve through which you are walking abuts the Rankokus Indian Reservation, and the walker here may well see the field on the reservation where real buffalo and horses are grazing or being put through their paces—an additional, and very welcome surprise.

Find your way back to the path (look for a small wooden bridge over the creek). The floodplain with its interesting growth of canary grasses and other water vegetation is particularly interesting in summertime. You'll find an amazing amount of plant life in these woods, including giant old trees, and the contorted shapes of many types of vines like Asiatic bittersweet, Japanese honeysuckle (one of those vines like kudzu that takes control), and frost grapes. (A proper list of birds, plants, and trees to look for can be had at the headquarters of the Audubon Society just across from the parking lot in a beautiful nineteenth-century farmhouse.)

Rancocas Nature Preserve is open dawn to dusk, at no charge. Telephone: 609-261-2495.

The **Palmyra Cove Nature Park** is located on the Delaware River in a most unlikely place for a park. It is just under the Tacony Bridge that goes into Philadelphia, where you might expect to find industry and parking lots. Instead, Burlington County has preserved a stretch of freshwater tidal marsh and river beachfront. (Pick up a self-guiding tour map from the box at the entrance.) It will take you on a strange loop, along the sandy shore of the Delaware with its view of urban industrialization in all directions (and a fair amount of flotsam and jetsam on the "beach"), into the interior of the park, where natural life abounds, birds sing, and you'll feel far removed from the bustle so close by.

Since 1940 the Army Corps of Engineers has dredged the river to some 40 feet deep to keep it open for shipping. The dredged silt now fills part of the original freshwater marsh on the shore, but it also provides a haven for wildlife and a habitat for birds. You'll come to a freshwater tidal marsh on a narrow spit of land (the ocean tides affect the level of the Delaware River as far north as Trenton), and here you'll see the tidal effects in the wetlands. Thus, you'll find Japanese honeysuckle growing on great old trees and delicate tall grasses rising out of the wetlands. Birds are singing everywhere, quite drowning out the low roar of traffic up on the bridge. There are some wonderful trees (some marked), including ailanthus and cottonwood and weeping willows and lots of berries (which also attract birds). Note: There is also poison ivy on this walk, so be careful!

Palmyra Cove Nature Park has no headquarters of its own. Open dawn to dusk. You can telephone the Burlington County Park System at 609-726-1191.

 The Barclay Farmstead Gardens, with its 32 acres of apple orchards, old farmhouse, herb garden, and ambience of a time long gone is a lovely place to walk. You can still imagine, as you walk through the grounds—particularly in spring when the trees are blossoming—just how appealing the place looked in the early 1800s. It has been beautifully restored and offers local residents a place to grow vegetables and flowers in an otherwise increasingly developed area.

The farm was first owned by a British family named Kay. In 1816 it was purchased by Joseph Thorn, who apparently constructed the 11-room house (now used for exhibitions and events). In 1826 the property was bought by a founder of Camden, Joseph Cooper, after whom its apples—Cooper's Russetings—were named. Among the various Cooper descendants were the Barclays, and they lived on the farm until the 1950s. Today, despite the surrounding development, the farmstead is still very inviting.

In addition to the orchard there is also a brief woodland trail on the property and an herb garden to enjoy, particularly in summertime. But if walking among apple blossoms is your pleasure, take this walk in springtime.

Barclay Gardens are open dawn to dusk daily. House is open Tuesday to Friday from 9 A.M. to 3 P.M. Telephone: 856-795-6225.

IN THE VICINITY
Rankokas Indian Reservation

The Renape Powhatan Indian Reservation is adjacent to the Rancocas Nature Preserve. It can be visited on its own for a variety of events (particularly on Memorial Day and Columbus Day, when there are such events as alligator wrestling), but at other times, too. There is a museum and animal and art shows and an ancestral village to visit. The reservation has nature trails, too.

Open Saturdays 10 A.M. to 3 P.M., or by appointment on Tuesdays and Thursdays. There is a fee. Telephone: 609-261-4747.

SOME ADDITIONAL GREEN SITES
TO EXPLORE

Assiniwikam Mountain

In Norvin Green State Park, this very pretty trail has a natural rock stair-case, blueberries, and wildflowers. Park at Camp Wyanokie, just north of Ringwood, or at Weis Ecology Center on Snake Den Road in Ringwood.

Atlantic County Park

Located at Estel Manor in the southern coastal area, this large (1,600-acre) park features Pine Barrens habitats, marshland, and fields, with some 15 miles of trails. There is also a nature center and greenhouse. Access is off Route 50, three miles south of Mays Landing.

Barnegat Light State Park

This popular 31-acre park surrounds the beloved Barnegat Lighthouse, "Old Barney," one of the most often pictured (and climbed) lighthouses in the nation. Access is via Route 72 to Long Beach Island on the Jersey shore.

Bearfort Ridge

This mountainous area is still well named, as bears are frequently sighted here. Dramatic rock formations and rugged terrain characterize this area in the northern highlands of the state. There is a well-known fire tower at the top of the trail. Access is from Warwick Turnpike, near Greenwood Lake.

Beaver Dam Creek County Park

As a change from beach scenery along the Atlantic coast, this 40-acre park in Point Pleasant, Ocean County, has boardwalks and trails into a wetland conservation area. Access is from Bridge Avenue in Point Pleasant on the Jersey shore.

Belleplain State Forest

This giant, 11,000-acre site is in northern Cape May County near the tip of New Jersey's coastal area. For hikers there is a boardwalk through wet-lands, a 6.5-mile trail around the 26-acre Lake Nummy, a former cranberry bog, and trails through acres of deep woods. Access is from Woodbine, Route 550 west.

Berlin Park

A 200-acre site in Camden County, this park along the Great Egg Harbor River includes an environmental study center and five miles of walking paths. Access is at the intersection of Routes 30, 534, and 561 in Berlin.

Carris Hill

This five-mile hike in northeastern New Jersey is for experienced hikers; it will take you through rugged terrain with many crossings over waterways and fine views throughout. Access is from Glenwild Avenue near Wanaque; you can leave your car at the Otter Hole Parking Area.

Cedar Swamp

This section of the Appalachian Trail is in High Point State Park in northern New Jersey. The dark, swampy setting is rich with mosses, ferns, and great trees. Access is from Route 23 at High Point, eight miles north of the town of Sussex.

Culvers Gap

This picturesque, rather rugged, site is located in the Delaware Water Gap National Park. Part of the Appalachian Trail, the hike to the Gap is mapped on material given out at the headquarters for the park, off Route 80.

Greenwood Forest and Pasadena Wildlife Management Area

The vast, more than 16,000-acre preserve in Ocean County includes many trails, a boardwalk through a cedar swamp, and three lakes. The northern entrance (and the boardwalk) are off Route 539 south of Whiting.

Governor Mountain's Cooper Union Trail

This lovely trail is part of Ringwood State Park in northern New Jersey, and its 3.5 miles will take you from Ringwood Manor through tall and beautiful woods toward Greenwood Lake. Access is at Ringwood State Park off Route 511.

Hartshorne Woods

Different from Hartshorne Woods Park, this 475-acre wilderness includes steep climbs to an overlook called Clay Court, with an impressive view of the Navesink River and surrounding Monmouth County. There are numerous marked trails that note their difficulty. Access is east of Keyport, south of Route 36; you'll find the entrance on Hartshorne Road in Locust.

Hoeferlin Memorial Trail

Located in the highlands of the state, this woodland trail leaves from the Ramapo Valley Country Reservation, crosses Ringwood State Park, and traverses part of Ramapo Mountain State Forest. Access is from Route 202, five miles north of Oakland; leave your car at Ramapo Valley County Reservation.

Jamesburg County Park

In the small town of Helmetta in Middlesex County, you'll find this 1,500-acre conservation area with its picturesque trails and sand roads. Access is from Route 522 in Helmetta, north of exit 8A on the N.J. Turnpike.

John A. Roebling Park

This 270-acre park is located in Hamilton Township in Mercer County. It is particularly noted for birdwatching on trails circling swamps, tidal marshes, and creeks. Access is south of Route 206 in Hamilton Township.

Mount Mitchill Scenic Overlook

The highest point on the Jersey shore—and indeed on the entire Atlantic coastline—this site is part of the Monmouth County Park System. This outing will provide you with a steep climb and marvelous views. Access is from the town of Atlantic Highlands on the northern Jersey coast.

Mullica River Wilderness

Near Batsto in the Pine Barrens, these trails on white-blazed paths take you through a remote region of the Barrens, with its odd and beautiful landscape of stunted trees and white sand paths. Access is in Wharton State Forest; park at the forest office in Batsto.

Pequannock Watershed

This site offers scenic hikes just south of Waywayanda State Park in the northern section of the state. Trails circle ponds and reservoirs, including the picturesque Buckabear Pond. Hemlocks and other great trees abound. Access is north of Newfoundland; pick up a trail map at Echo Lake Road, off Route 23, south of Clinton Road.

Raccoon Ridge, A.M.C. Mohican Outdoor Center

A rocky, challenging five-mile hike in the Kittatinny Mountains, this walk is not for everyone. These mountains in the northwestern corner of the state are quite rugged, and this walk is beautiful but tough. If viewing hawks is your thing, this is the place to be. Access is from Route 94 north of Route 80 at Jacksonburg.

Rattlesnake Swamp

This site, located in the Kittatinny Mountains in northwestern New Jersey, is a remote and beautiful one. Walking here offers trails through forests of tall hemlocks, with a profusion of rhododendrons in late spring. If you walk five miles, you'll come to Catfish Pond. Access is from the Appalachian Trail north of Blairstown; take Route 94 to County Route 602.

Reinhardt Preserve

The Sussex County preserve includes marshland, a wooded swamp, a hemlock glen, and several informal hiking trails. This is a good place to spot wildlife. Access is from Clove Road (Route 653) near High Point State Park.

Rifle Camp Park

Located in West Paterson, this is a 153-acre park with a nature center and an astronomical observatory. Also here is a bird blind and several miles of nature trails. One picnic area is designed especially for the handicapped. Access is from Squirrelwood Road off Route 80 in West Paterson.

Troy Meadows Natural Area

This 400-acre area includes freshwater marsh, swamp and floodplain, and several hiking trails. It is a rare-species area and is recommended for bird-watching. Access is from Troy Hills–Parsippany, off Route 80.

Verona Park

The site has three miles of trails in a 54-acre area, with a nice sized lake and rowboats and paddle boats to rent. Access is south of Route 506 (Bloomfiled Avenue) and east of Lakeside Avenue in Verona, Essex County.

Weequahic County Park

This 300-acre park has eight miles of walking trails and a large lake right in the city of Newark. Access is from Route 22 on Elizabeth Avenue in Newark.

Wyanokie Circular Trail, Norvin Green State Forest

This trail offers not only a beautiful woodland setting with tall hemlocks and giant boulders, but an abandoned mine, which you can explore (bring your flashlight) if you wish. The trail also meanders to the picturesque Blue Mine Brook. Access is from the Weis Ecology Center at Snake Den Road in Ringwood.

CHOOSING AN OUTING

Place	Walk Number
ART SITES	
Peters Valley Craft Center	13
Millbrook Craft Village	14
Princeton University Campus	22
Grounds for Sculpture	24
Georgian Court College	28
Sculpture Garden at Burlington County College	31
Wheaton Village	38
BEACH WALKS	
Sandy Hook	25
Island Beach State Park	29
Cattus Island	29
Brigantine Island	34
Seven Mile Beach, Avalon	34
Hereford Inlet	35
Cape May Point State Park	36
Higbee Beach Wildlife Management Area	36
Moores Beach	37
East Point Light House	37
BEST BIRDING	
Celery Farm Natural Area	2
Ramapo County Reservation	2
Overpeck Park	3
Palisades Walk	3
Scherman-Hoffman Sanctuaries	7
Great Swamp Wildlife Refuge	7
Lord Stirling Park	7
Cora Hartshorn Arboretum	8
South Mountain Reservation	8
Hammond Wildlife Trail	11
Pyramid Mountain	11

Place	Walk Number
Sparta Mountain	12
Delaware-Raritan Canal	20
Sandy Hook	25
Cheesequake State Park	26
Turkey Swamp	27
Owl Haven	27
Forsythe National Wildlife Refuge	33
Great Bay Boulevard Wildlife Management Area	33
Manahawkin Wildlife Natural Area	33
Holgate	33
Brigantine Island	34
Cape May Bird and Migratory Refuge	36
Cape May Bird Observatory	36
Higbee Beach Wildlife Management Area	36
Parvin State Park	38
Supawna Meadows National Wildlife Refuge	39
Rancocas Natural Preserve	40
BEST TOWN AND COUNTY PARKS	
Branch Brook Park	5
Lord Stirling Park	7
Rahway River Park	8
Louis Morris County Park	10
Loantaka Brook Reservation	10
Tourne County Park	11
Old Troy Park	11
Black River County Park	16
Marquand Park	21
Crosswicks Creek Park	24

Place	Walk Number
Veterans Park	24
Tatum Park	26
Hartshorne Woods Park	26
Ocean County Park	28
Smithville County Park	31
Heritage Park	34

BIKING

Place	Walk Number
Patriot's Path	7
Loantaka Brook Reservation	10
Jenny Jump State Forest	11
Round Valley State Park	17
Delaware-Raritan Canal	20
Veterans Park	24
Sandy Hook	25
Hartshorne Woods Park	26
Manasquan Reservoir	27
Ocean County Park and nearby lakes	28
Island Beach State Park	29
Cattus Island	29
Forsythe National Wildlife Refuge	33
Great Bay Boulevard Wildlife Management Area	33
Manahawkin Wildlife Natural Area	33
Egg Island	37
Parvin State Park	38

COLLEGE CAMPUSES

Place	Walk Number
Rutgers University	21
Princeton University	22
Georgian Court College	28
Ocean County College Arboretum	29
Burlington County College	31

ESPECIALLY GOOD FOR CHILDREN

Place	Walk Number
Ringwood Manor	1
McFaul Environmental Center	2

Place	Walk Number
Flatrock Brook Natural Center	3
Paterson Great Falls	3
Lambert Castle	4
Liberty State Park	6
Great Swamp National Wildlife Refuge	7
Lord Stirling Park	7
South Mountain Reservation	8
Willowwood Arboretum	9
Morristown National Historic Park	10
Old Troy Park	11
Waterloo Village	12
Swartswood State Park	13
Tillman Ravine	13
Delaware Water Gap	14
Pequest Trout Hatchery	15
Hacklebarney State Park	16
Grounds for Sculpture	24
Sandy Hook	25
Poricy Park	25
Monmouth Battlefield	27
Allaire Deserted Village	27
Island Beach and Cattus Island	29
Dot and Brooks Evert Memorial Nature Trail	31
Bauma's Farm Corn Maze	31
Heritage Park	34
Wetlands Institute	35
Hereford Inlet	35
Cape May	36
Parvin State Park	38
Wheaton Village	38
Red Bank Battlefield	39

FEDERAL AND STATE PARKS

Place	Walk Number
Ringwood State Park	1
Wawayanda State Park	1
Long Pond Ironworks	1
Liberty State Park	6
High Point State Park	13
Swartswood State Park	13

Place	Walk Number
Delaware Water Gap National Recreation Area	14
Worthington State Forest	14
Allamuchy State Park	15
Stephens State Park	15
Hacklebarney State Park	16
Voorhees State Park	17
Round Valley State Park	17
Princeton Battlefield State Park	22
Washington Crossing State Park	23
Cheesequake State Park	26
Island Beach State Park	29
Double Trouble State Park	30
Wharton State Forest	32
Bass River State Forest	32
Forsythe National Wildlife Refuge	33
Corson's Inlet State Park	35
Cape May Point State Park	36
Parvin State Park	38
Fort Mott State Park	39

FORESTS

Place	Walk Number
Garrett Mountain Reservation	4
Mills Reservation	5
Watchung Reservation	8
Jenny Jump State Forest	12
Stokes State Forest	13
Swartswood State Park	13
Hacklebarney State Park	16
Sourland Mountain Preserve	19
Frank Helyar Woods	21
Huber Woods	25
Double Trouble State Park	30
Wharton State Forest	32
Bass River State Forest	32
Parvin State Park	38

GARDENS AND ARBORETUMS

Place	Walk Number
Skylands Botanic Garden	1
Van Vleck Gardens	5

Place	Walk Number
Presby Memorial Iris Garden	5
Cora Hartshorn Arboretum	8
Cross Estate Gardens	9
Leonard J. Buck Garden	9
Bamboo Brook Gardens	9
Willowwood Arboretum	9
Frelinghuysen Arboretum	10
Delbarton Gardens	10
Hunterdon County Arboretum	17
Doris Duke Gardens	19
Colonial Park	20
Rutgers Display Gardens	21
Prospect Gardens, Princeton University	22
Sayen Gardens	24
Holmdel Arboretum	26
Thompson Park	26
Deep Cut Gardens	26
Sambol-Citta Arboretum	29
Waldor Orchids	34
Scotland Run County Park	38
Barclay Farmstead Gardens	40

HISTORIC SITES

Place	Walk Number
Long Pond Iron Works	1
Ringwood Manor	1
Lambert Castle	4
Bloomfield Cemetery	5
Liberty State Park	6
Morristown National Historic Park	10
Patriot's Path	7, 10
Waterloo Village	12
Princeton Cemetery	22
Princeton Battlefield State Park	22
Prallsville Mill	23
Historic Walnford	24
Twin Lights	25
Fort Hancock	25
Long Street Farm	26
Allaire Deserted Village	27

Place	Walk Number
Monmouth Battlefield	27
Cranberry Village	30
Batsto Village	32
Cape May Lighthouse & State Park	36
East Point Light House	37
Wheaton Village	38
Red Bank Battlefield	39
Fort Mott State Park	39
Finn's Point Red Range Light	39
Rankokas Indian Reservation	40

ISLAND WALKS

Place	Walk Number
Cattus Island	29
Island Beach	29
Long Beach Island	33
Brigantine Island	34
Egg Island	37

MARSHES

Place	Walk Number
Great Swamp National Wildlife Refuge	7
Poricy Park	25
Cheesequake State Park	26
Turkey Swamp	27
Cattus Island	29
Double Trouble State Park	30
Corson's Inlet State Park	33
Wetlands Institute	35
East Point Lighthouse	37
Egg Island	37
Palmyra Cove Nature Park	40

MOUNTAINS AND VISTAS

Place	Walk Number
Campgaw Mountain Ski Area	2
Palisades Interstate Park	3
Garrett Mountain Reservation	4
South Mountain Reservoir	8
Watchung Reservation	8
Pyramid Mountain	11
Tourne County Park	11
Sparta Mountain	12
High Point State Park and Monument Trail	13
Delaware Water Gap	14
Sourland Mountain Preserve	19
Wharton State Forest	32

NATURE CENTERS AND PRESERVES

Place	Walk Number
Fyke Nature Center	2
Ramapo County Reservation	2
James A. McFaul Environmental Center	2
Flat Rock Brook Nature Center	3
Tenafly Nature Center	3
Great Swamp National Wildlife Refuge	7
South Mountain Nature Center	8
Watchung Reservation	8
Loantaka Brook Reservation	10
Pyramid Mountain	11
Ken Lockwood Gorge Wildlife Management Area	17
Sourland Mountain Preserve	19
Plainsboro Preserve	21
Dot and Brooks Evert Memorial Nature Trail	31
Sawmill Nature Center	32
Cape May Migratory Bird Refuge	36
Higbee Beach Wildlife Management Area	36
Rancocas Nature Preserve	40
Palmyra Cove Nature Park	40

RAIL TRAILS

Place	Walk Number
Rockaway Valley Railroad	10
Sussex Branch Trail	12
Karamac Road Trail	14
Paulinskill Valley Trail	14
Black River Management Area Rail Trail	16
Cooper Mill Rail Trail	16

Place	Walk Number
Kingston Branch Loop Trail	20
Delaware and Raritan Canal State Park	23
Bull's Island	23
Freehold and Jamesburg Rail Trail	27
Pemberton Rail Trail	31

VINEYARDS, ORCHARDS, AND CORN MAZES

Place	Walk Number
Alba Vineyard	18
Amwell Valley Vineyard	18
Unionville Vineyards	18
Little Acres Corn Maze	23
Battleview Orchards	27
Bauma's Farm Corn Maze	31

WATERSIDE WALKS

Place	Walk Number
Shepherd Lake	1
Palisades Shore Path	3
Paterson Great Falls	4
Liberty State Park	6
Rahway River Park	8
Sunrise Lake	10
Birchwood Lake	11
Buttermilk Falls	13
Swartswood State Park	13
Delaware Water Gap	14
Merrill Creek Reservation	15
Deer Park Pond	15
Black River	16
Delaware and Raritan Canal	20, 23
Plainsboro Preserve	21
Washington Crossing State Park	23
Sandy Hook	25
Manasquan Reservation	27
Lake Shenandoah Park	28
Lake Carasaljo	28
Island Beach State Park	29
Cattus Island	29

Place	Walk Number
Double Trouble State Park	30
Smithville County Park	31
Forsythe Wildlife Management Area	33
Manahawkin Wildlife Natural Area	33
Brigantine Island	34
Heritage Park	34
Corson's Inlet	35
Hereford Inlet	35
Cape May	36

WHEELCHAIR AND STROLLER ACCESS

Place	Walk Number
Flat Rock Brook Nature Center	3
Lord Stirling Park	7
Rahway River Park	8
Frelinghuysen Arboretum	10
Swartswood State Park	13
Paulinskill Valley Trail	14
Delaware and Raritan Canal State Park	20, 23
Cattus Island	29
Cooper Environmental Center	29
Pemberton Rail Trail	31
Forsythe National Wildlife Refuge	33
Hereford Inlet	35
Cape May Point State Park	36
Wheaton Village	38

WILDFLOWERS

Place	Walk Number
Celery Farm Natural Area	2
Ramapo County Reservation	2
Leonard J. Buck Garden	9
Wildwood Arboretum	9
Hammond Wildflower Trail	11
Plainsboro Preserve	21
Bowman's Hill Wildflower Preserve	23
Poricy Park	25
Cheesequake State Park	26

PHOTO CREDITS

Photos by the authors, except as follows: Chapter 1, Department of Environmental Protection, Bureau of Parks, courtesy of Elbertus Prol, photographer. Chapters 3, 4, 11, courtesy of Peter Gall, photographer. Chapters 5, 7, 12, 14, 20, 23, 26, 30, 37, photos by Barrow, courtesy of the New Jersey Commerce and Economic Growth Commission. Chapter 10, courtesy of Dr. Paul Diveny, O.S.B., Delbarton School. Chapter 15, photo by Jim Mershon, courtesy of Merrill Creek Reservation. Chapter 18, courtesy of Unionville Vineyards. Chapter 22, courtesy of Sue Rodgers, photographer. Chapters 27, 35, courtesy of New Jersey Heritage Trail Route. Chapter 28, courtesy of Michael Gross, Ph.D., photographer, Georgian Court College. Chapters 29, 32, courtesy of Judy Travisano, photographer. Chapters 34, 36, courtesy of Cape May County Department of Tourism. Chapter 38, courtesy of Wheaton Village. Cover photo, courtesy of Jim Mershon, courtesy of Merrill Creek Reservation.

INDEX

Place	Walk Number	Place	Walk Number
Absecon	34	Cape May County	35, 36
Alba Vineyard	18	Cape May Migratory Bird Refuge	36
Allaire Deserted Village	27	Cape May Point State Park	36
Allamuchy State Park	15	Cattus Island	29
Amwell Valley Vineyard	18	Cedar Grove	5
Apple Pie Hill Fire Tower	32	Celery Farm Natural Area	2
Atlantic County	33, 34	Cheesequake State Park	26
Avalon	34	Cherry Hill	41
		Chester	16
Bamboo Brook Gardens	9	Clayton	38
Barclay Farmstead Gardens	40	Clinton	17
Bass River State Forest	32	Colonial Park	20
Batona Trail	32	Cooper Mill	16
Batsto Lake	32	Cooper Environmental Center	29
Batsto Village	32	Cora Hartshorn Arboretum	8
Battleview Orchards	27	Corson's Inlet State Park	35
Bauma's Corn Maze	31	Cresswick Creek Park	24
Belleville	5	Cranberry Village	30
Bergen County	2, 3	Cross Estate Gardens	9
Bernardsville	9	Cumberland County	37, 38
Birchwood Lake	11		
Black River County Park	16	Deep Cut Gardens	26
Black River Wildlife Management Area	16	Deer Park Pond	15
Bloomfield Cemetery	5	Delaware and Raritan Canal State Park	20, 23
Boonton	11	Delaware River	18, 23, 39, 40
Bowman's Hill State Wildflower Preserve	23	Delaware Water Gap	14
Branch Brook Park	5	Delbarton Gardens	10
Brigantine Island	34	Doris Duke Gardens	19
Bull's Island	23	Dot and Brooks Evert Memorial Nature Trail	31
Burlington County	31, 32, 41	Double Trouble State Park	30
Buttermilk Falls	13	Dryden Kuser Natural Area	13
		Dunnfield Hollow Trail	14
Campgaw Mountain Ski Area	2		
Cape May Bird Observatory	36		

Place	Walk Number
East Point Light House	37
Edwin S. Forsythe National Wildlife Refuge	33
Egg Island	37
Englewood	3
Essex County	5, 8
Finn's Point Rear Range Light	39
Flat Rock Brook Nature Center	3
Forsythe National Wildlife Refuge	33
Fort Hancock	25
Fort Mott State Park	39
Frank G. Helyar Woods	21
Freehold and Jamesburg Rail Trail	27
Frelinghuysen Arboretum	10
Fyke Nature Center	2
Garrett Mountain Reservation	4
Georgian Court College	28
Glassboro Wildlife Management Area	38
Gloucester County	39, 40
Great Bay Blvd. Wildlife Management Area	33
Great Swamp National Wildlife Refuge	7
Greenwich	37
Grounds for Sculpture	24
Hacklebarney State Park	16
Hamilton Township	24
Hammond Wildlife Trail	11
Hartshorn Arboretum	8
Hartshorne Woods Park	26
Hereford Inlet	35
Heritage Park	34
Higbee Beach Wildlife Management Area	36
High Point State Park	13
Holgate	33
Holmdel Park and Arboretum	26

Place	Walk Number
Huber Woods	25
Hudson County	6
Hudson River Shore	3
Hunterdon County	17, 18
Hunterdon County Arboretum	17
Island Beach State Park	29
Jenny Jump State Forest	12
Jersey Shore	25, 26, 29, 34, 35, 36
Jockey Hollow Encampment	10
Karamac Road Trail	14
Kay Environmental Center	16
Ken Lockwood Gorge Wildlife Management Area	17
Kingston Branch Loop Trail	20
Lake Carasaljo	28
Lake Shenandoah Park	28
Lakewood	28
Lambert Castle	4
Lebanon State Forest	30
Leonard J. Buck Garden	9
Leonia	3
Liberty State Park	6
Linwood	34
Little Acres Corn Maze	23
Loantaka Brook Reservation	10
Long Beach Island	29
Long Pond Ironworks State Park	1
Lord Stirling Park	7
Louis Morris County Park	10
Manahawkin Wildlife Natural Area	33
Manasquan Reservoir	27
Marquand Park	22
Mauriceville	37
McFaul Environmental Center	2

Place	Walk Number	Place	Walk Number
Mercer County	22, 23, 24	Pine Barrens	30
Merrill Creek Reservoir	15	Plainsboro Preserve	21
Milford	18	Poricy Park	25
Millburn	8	Prallsville Mill	23
Mills Reservation	5	Presby Memorial Iris Garden	5
Millville	38	Princeton Battlefield State Park	22
Monmouth Battlefield	27		
Monmouth County	25, 26, 27	Princeton Cemetery	22
Montclair	5	Princeton University	22
Monument Trail	13	Prospect Gardens	22
Moores Beach	37	Pyramid Mountain Natural Historical Area	11
Morris County	7, 9, 10, 11, 16		
Morristown National Historic Park	10	Rahway River Park	8
		Ramapo County Reservation	2
Mountain Lakes	11	Rancocas Nature Preserve	40
Mount Tammany	14	Rankokas Indian Reservation	40
		Red Bank Battlefield	39
North Wildwood	35	Ringoes	18
		Ringwood Manor	1
Ocean County	28, 29, 30, 33	Ringwood State Park	1
		Round Valley State Park	17
Ocean County College Sambol-Citta Arboretum	29	Rutgers Display Gardens	21
Ocean County Park	28	Salem County	38, 39
Old Troy Park	11	Sandy Hook	25
Overpeck Park	3	Sayen Gardens	24
Owl Haven	27	Scherman-Hoffman Wildlife Sanctuaries	7
Pakim Pond	30	Scotland Run Park	38
Palisades Interstate Park	3	Seven Mile Beach	34
Palisades Shore Path	3	Shepherd Lake	1
Palmyra Cove Nature Park	40	Skylands Botanical Garden	1
Parsippany-Troy Hills	11	Smithville County Park	31
Parvin State Park	38	Somerset County	19, 20, 21
Passaic County	1, 4	Sourland Mountain Preserve	19
Paterson Great Falls	4	South Mountain Reservation	8
Patriot's Path	7, 10	Sparta Mountain	12
Paulinskill Valley Trail	14	Speedwell Park	10
Pemberton Rail Trail	31	Stephens State Park	15
Pequest Trout Hatchery	15	Stokes State Forest	13
Peters Valley	13	Stone Harbor	35

Place	Walk Number
Sunrise Lake	10
Supawna Meadows National Wildlife Refuge	39
Sussex Branch Rail Trail	12
Sussex County	12, 13
Swartswood State Park	13
Tatum Park	26
Tenafly Nature Center	3
Thompson Park	26
Tillman Ravine	13
Toms River	29
Tourne County Park	11
Traction Line Recreational Trail	10
Turkey Swamp	27
Twin Lights	25
Unionville Vineyards	18
Van Campens Glen	14
Van Vleck Gardens	5

Place	Walk Number
Veterans Park	24
Voorhees State Park	17
Waldor Orchids	34
Walnford	24
Warren County	14, 15
Washington Crossing State Park	23
Watchung Reservation	8
Wells County Park	3
Waterloo Village	12
Wawayanda State Park	1
Weehawken	6
Wells Mills County Park	30
Wetlands Institute	35
Wharton State Forest	32
Wheaton Village	38
Whitesbog Village	30
Willowwood Arboretum	9
Worthington State Forest	14

ABOUT THE AUTHORS

Lucy D. Rosenfeld and Marina Harrison have written six previous guide-books together. Among them are walking guides to public gardens, cultural sites, and natural wonders. Lifelong friends, they enjoy exploring new places, revisiting favorite venues, as well as writing about them for other walkers and nature lovers.

Lucy D. Rosenfeld is the author of numerous books on art and cultural history, including recent works on American sculpture and architecture. Marina Harrison has been a writer and editor for a major publishing firm for many years.